FRANCIS ISABELLA DUBERLY

I0568937

THE WAR OF ROGER & FANNY
FROM THE DEPARTURE OF THE ARMY FROM ENGLAND
IN APRIL 1854, TO THE FALL OF SEBASTOPOL

WITNESS TO HISTORY 001

SOLDIERSHOP
PUBLISHING

AUTHOR:

Frances Isabella ("Fanny") Duberly (27 September 1829 – 19 November 1902) was an British Cavalry officer's wife, she kept a journal of her experiences in the Crimean War, including the Battle of Balaklava and the charge of the Light Brigade. It was published to great acclaim in 1856. A second book followed a few years later, giving her account of the suppression of the Sepoy Mutiny (the Indian Rebellion of 1857). Her husband, Captain Henry Duberly, was paymaster to the 8th Royal Irish Hussars, part of the British light cavalry that took part in the Charge of the Light Brigade. Duberley's journal of her time in the Crimea was published as Journal Kept During the Russian War. It not only includes eye-witness accounts, but is also a record of gossip and rumours circulating in the British Army.

PUBLISHING NOTE

WITNESS TO HISTORY

Our book series of history, based on eyewitnesses, or the great storytellers and war correspondents of the great events of world history: battles, sieges, military campaigns, but also travels and discoveries. New books from old books and completely revised and illustrated by Soldiershop!

To my daughter Anny

ISBN: 9788893271103   1st edition July 2016 Ebook edition ISBN 9788896519820

Title: - **The war of Roger & Fanny (WTH-001)**
by Frances Isabella Duberly (1829-1902). Revised and enriched by Luca Stefano Cristini (note & illustrations) Editor: Soldiershop publishing - Cover & Art Design: Luca S. Cristini.

Cover: The Roger Fenton's photographic van in Crimea 1854

PREFACE

Fanny was quite a girl, but also a writer of considerable talent. Maligned by some of her contemporaries because she didn't quite fit in with the Victorian image of what a 'lady' should be, she did things her way and wrote about them in a vivid, lively way, bringing the Crimean War to gut-wrenching life in a way no history book can.

She was there for the duration, saw the Charge of the Light Brigade, walked through the ruins of Sebastopol and didn't hesitate to say what she thought. Admired, parodied but never ignored, Fanny Duberly was a force of nature and a woman out of her time.

The diary is linked by well-chosen excerpts from her letters and brief historical notes, putting what Fanny is saying into its proper context. We have enriched this terrific book with several Roger Fenton'images of Crimean war in colour, to offer to you something more wonderful!!

This book is based on *"the Journal Kept During The Russian War"* by Frances Isabella Locke Duberly. London: Longman, Brown, Green, and Longmans, 1856. No effort has been made to modernize or standardize the spelling used in the original text.

Luca Stefano Cristini

Original Editor's note

The writer of this Diary accompanied her husband, an officer in the 8th Hussars, who left England, with his regiment, on the breaking out of the war, and she is now with him in the Crimea.

Original Preface

I am aware of many deficiencies in this Journal. It was kept under circumstances of great difficulty.
I have always put down information as I received it, as nearly as possible in the words of my informant, in matters which I did not myself witness. I have endeavoured to keep free from comment or remark, thinking it best to allow he facts to speak for themselves.
When this Journal was first commenced I had no intention whatever of publishing it; nor should I have done so now, had it not been for the kind interest manifested in it by many of my friends.

CONTENTS:

TURKEY IN DANGER.

" Now all the youth of England are on fire.
And silken dalliance in the wardrobe lies;
Now thrive the armourers, and Honour's thought
Reigns solely in the breast of every man."

" Je vais où le vent me mène,
Sans me plaindre ou m'effrayer.
Je vais où va toute chose;
Où va la feuille de Rose,
Et la feuille de Laurier."

TO THE SOLDIERS AND SAILORS OF THE CRIMEAN EXPEDITION THIS JOURNAL IS DEDICATED
BY AN EYE WITNESS OF THEIR CHIVALROUS VALOUR AND THEIR HEROIC FORTITUDE,

▲ Two English cavalryman of the British expedition force in Crimea (1854-1855)

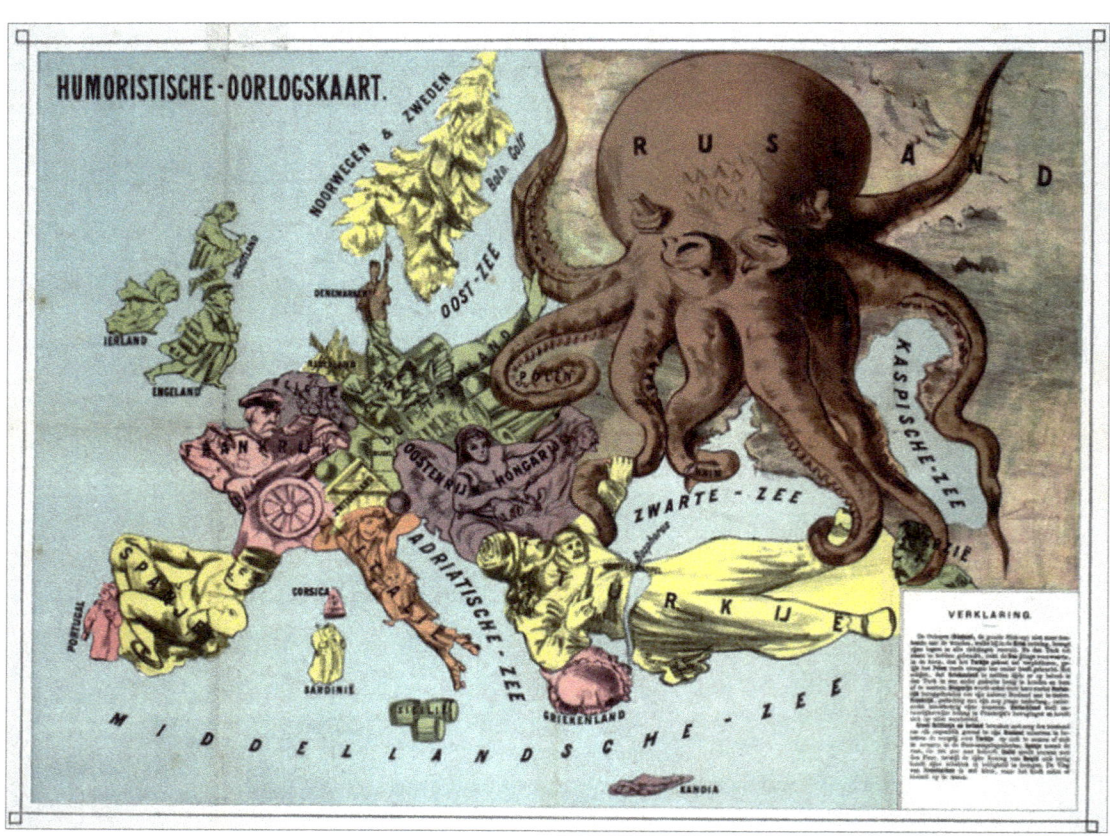

▲ Satirical Map of Europe during the Crimean War

CHAPTER I

THE
VOYAGE

▲ Three Highlander soldiers 1854-55.

THE VOYAGE

"The sails were fill'd, and light the fair winds blew,
As glad to waft us from our native home;
And fast the white rocks faded from our view,
And soon were lost in circumambient foam."
BYRON

Monday, April 24th, 1854. – Left the New London Inn at Exeter at ten o'clock in the evening, with sad heart and eyes full of tears. The near approach of this long voyage, and the prospect of unknown trials and hardships to be endured for I know not how long, overwhelmed me at the last moment; and the remembrance of dear friends left behind, whom I never more might return to see, made me shrink most nervously from the new life on which I was to embark. We reached the Royal Hotel at Plymouth at midnight, after a bitterly cold journey.

Tuesday, 25th. – After making a few purchases necessary for our comfort during the voyage, we embarked about three o'clock on board the *"Shooting Star,"* lying in the Plymouth dockyard; and towards evening, amid indescribable hurry, confusion, and noise, we weighed our anchor, and dropped down the river, where we lay till three o'clock on Wednesday morning; and then, with a fair and gentle breeze, and every prospect of a prosperous voyage, we stood out to sea.

Friday, 28th. – The breeze, which had been gradually freshening during yesterday, increased last night. I, sick and almost helpless in my cabin, was told the disastrous news that both the mizen-top and main-top gallant-masts were carried away; that fragments of the wreck – masts, ropes, and spars – strewed the deck: one poor fellow was lying seriously injured, having broken his leg, and crushed the bone.

Saturday, 29th. – Weak and nervous, I staggered up on deck, to see it strewn with spars, ropes, and blocks. During the night the gale had fearfully increased, and the morning sun found two of our poor horses dead. The groans of the boy, who was lying in one of the cabins, and the gloom caused by the death of our horses, threw us all into depressed spirits, which were not cheered by looking at the ugly, broken mast aloft. I heartily thank God, who brought us safely through last night's gale. Although weakened almost to delirium by sea-sickness and awed by the tremendous force of wind and sea, I could not but exult in the magnificent sailing of our noble ship, which bounded over the huge waves like a wild hunter springing at his fences, and breasted her gallant way at the rate of sixteen knots an hour.

Sunday, 30th. – How unlike the quiet Sundays at home! How sadly we thought of them – of pleasant walks to church, through sunny fields and shady lanes! After we had read the service, Henry and I went on deck, and sat there quietly. The wind had dropped to a dead calm; and our good ship, as though resting after her late effort, dozed lazily along at barely two knots an hour Towards evening, we saw several whales and porpoises, and phosphorescent lights gleamed like stars on the calm, dark sea.

Monday, May 1st. – The wind still very quiet, and our ship hardly making any way.

Tuesday, 2nd. – We signalled a vessel which, after much delay, replied that she was the *"Blundel,"* from Portsmouth, bound to Gallipoli. At ten o'clock to-night we arrived off Gibraltar. For some hours previously we were in sight of the Spanish coast; and, notwithstanding the lateness of the hour, the clear atmosphere and brilliant moon enabled us to discern the town of Gibraltar and the Rock rising behind it. It was a cause of much disappointment to us that we had not passed it earlier, as we hoped to have conveyed to our friends at home the news of our safe arrival thus far. Another horse died from inanition, having eaten nothing since he came on board.

Wednesday, 3rd. – An almost entire calm. Our lazy ship scarcely vouchsafed to move at all. Such a glorious day, succeeded by a night which realised all one's dreams of the sweet south! – the Spanish and African coasts still visible, and on the former, mountains capped with snow. We put up an awning on the deck, as the heat was very great. During the night, however, a fresh breeze sprung up, filling our flapping sails, and bearing us on at the rate of fifteen knots an hour.

Thursday, 4th. – The breeze continued, and our good ship went cheerily on her course. A fourth horse died last night. They tell me he went absolutely mad, and raved himself to death. The hold where our horses are stowed, although considered large and airy, appears to me horrible beyond words.
The slings begin to gall the horses under the shoulder and breastbone; and the heat and bad atmosphere must be felt to be understood. Every effort to alleviate their sufferings is made; their nostrils are spunged with vinegar, which is also scattered in the hold. Our three horses bear it bravely, but they are immediately under a hatchway where they get air.

Friday, 5th. – A day of much sorrow and suffering to me, as I was awoke by our servant (Connell) coming to our door at seven o'clock, and saying that the *"Grey Horse"* – *"Missus's Horse"* – my own dear horse, was very ill. Henry ran to him directly, and after examining him, fancied his attack was different from that of the others, and that he might live. How deeply one becomes attached to a favourite horse! Never was a more perfect creature, with faultless action, faultless mouth, and faultless temper.

Saturday, 6th. – My horse still lives, and they tell me he is a thought easier; but last night was most unfavourable to him, there being a fresh wind and rolling sea. During the forenoon I came on deck, heavy at heart.
We passed the island of Galita, of volcanic formation and rocky appearance: it appears to be covered with a rusty brown moss. During the afternoon we exchanged signals with vessels which had been respectively twenty-eight, seventeen, and fourteen days at sea. We have been ten.

Sunday, 7th. – A lovely morning, and a quiet sea. Although the *"Shooting Star"* makes but seven knots an hour, we hope to arrive at Malta by dark. Had the wind held, we should have been off the town in time for afternoon service. My letters are ready for S., W., and Mrs. F. Would that we could receive news from home! I hear we passed the Island of Pantelaria this morning, but was not on deck in time to see it; indeed, I had no heart for the distractions of outward objects, for my horse, though he still lives, is at the point of death.

Monday, 8th. – We were awoke at four o'clock by the sound of a matin bell, and knew by it that we were off Malta. Looking through the stern windows, we found ourselves at anchor in the harbour; the massive fortifications bristling with guns were close on either side of us, as we lay quiet and motionless on the waveless sea. At eight o'clock Henry went on deck, and soon after returning, put his arms round me, and I knew that my darling horse was out of pain! Henry went ashore with Captain Fraser, and, amid the sultry heat, sweltered up the *"Nix mangiare"* stairs, and through the blinding streets of the town.
At ten we received orders to put to sea forthwith; but the wind lay ahead of us, and at five we were barely moving out of port. Shortly after, when the calm evening was dressed in all the gorgeous colours of a southern sunset, and whilst the military calls were sounding those stirring notes he loved to hear, my good horse was lowered to his rest among the nautili and wondrous seaflowers which floated round the ship.
A small French brig, containing a detachment of the Chasseurs d'Afrique, lay becalmed close to us. They told us that their vessel was one of 150 tons; that they had twenty-eight horses on board, and had lost none, although they provided no stalls for them, but huddled them into the hold as closely as they could stow them away.

Tuesday, 9th. – Our orders are to proceed to Cape Matapan, where, if the wind should be against us, a steamer will tow us to Scutari. Some of our crew, having bought spirits from the bumboats off Malta, became mutinous, and several passed the night in irons.

Friday, 12th. – Last night ominous banks of clouds loaded the horizon, and soon proved the truth of my quotation – *"There's tempest in yon horned moon, And lightning in yon cloud."* A hurricane of wind thundered in our rigging, and a deluge of rain came down. Endeavouring to make head against the gale, Captain Fraser tried our good ship to the utmost, but was at last obliged to let her drive before the storm It was a fearful night to us who are unaccustomed to the sea; the rolling was very heavy and wearisome. Neither Henry nor I undressed all night. To-day has been a day of as much suffering as I ever wish to experience.

Sick incessantly, too weak to turn, I was lying towards night almost unconscious, when I was roused by a most tremendous roll. The ship had heeled over till her deck was under water. Candlesticks, falling from the table, rolled at their leisure into the corners. Captain Fraser rushed on deck, Captain Tomkinson into the hold, where every horse was down, one being pitched half over the manger. I was shot from the stern locker, on which I was lying, to the far corner of my cabin, and every box and portmanteau came crushing over me.

▲ The great Alliance for the Eastern war.

Saturday, 13th. – Happily, the violent motion abated during the night, though the thunder and lightning were terrific. And this is the *"Sweet South! whose sky rains roses and violets, and whose weary, fragrant heat, combined with gorgeous colours, dazzles the senses so that one feels like a phœnix burning on spice wood."* This is all very fine, but Singleton Fontenoy must have been more fortunate in his time of year.

To me, for the last three days, the Mediterranean has been arid and sickly as the first approach of fever – heaving, nauseating, as the deadly approach of plague. Those who are good sailors may linger over it if they will. Give me the smallest house in England, with a greenhouse and a stable, and I will sigh no more for the violet waves of a Mediterranean sea, nor the brilliant stars of a sometimes golden heaven.

Sunday, 14th. – Ran on deck to take my first longing look at Greece. We were close under the Arcadian shore, about four miles from the Island of Stamphane. The high, bold coast lay hazy and crowned with misty clouds in the early sunlight. I watched for an hour, my mind dreaming poetic fancies: *"I, too, have been in Arcadia."* A brilliant day coloured the blue waves once more. We had service for all hands on deck. Mr. Coull, the Admiralty agent, officiated; and being somewhat unaccustomed to acting chaplain, he read the prayer for Queen Adelaide straight through.

Monday, 15th. – Almost a calm. We sighted the *"Maryanne,"* with Major De Salis and a detachment of 8th Hussars on board. She sailed a week before us, and our having overtaken her is a great triumph to our ship. The Messenian coast lay close to us all day – snowcapped and cloud-wreathed mountains lying in a half indistinct and dreamy haze, a very Eleusinian mystery in themselves.

Tuesday, 16th. – After dark we passed the Straits of Cerigo; and all this morning have been gliding amongst the islands of the Archipelago, leaving Rock St. George upon our left, and the fertile and beautifully cultivated Zea on our right. They lay in beauteous sleep upon the bosom of the ocean, in colouring half intense, half languid, like the tints of the dog-rose and wild violet. Silently and swiftly our good ship held her way. We sighted the *"Echinga,"* which had sailed ten days before us, but we did not overtake her before nightfall (star-rise would be a better word); but we followed on her track as surely as evil destiny follows a foredoomed soul.

Wednesday, 17th. – As I write we are off Mitylene, an apparently uncultivated island, but full of beauty of outline and colour nevertheless; and after coasting for two hours the fertile and well-wooded shores of Asia, we came to the narrow passage between Tenedos and the mainland. This passage is dangerous, from a reef of rocks; but we spanked through it at eleven knots, closely followed by the *"Echinga,"* while they saluted us from the batteries. Three hours later, our favouring breeze had whispered its own lullaby, and we were lying helpless and becalmed at the mouth of the Dardanelles.

A strong current, acting on the ship, swung her round broadside to the forts. The glory of the sunset, the gaily painted little Turkish vessels, with the brilliant fez and long pipes of the sailors, the still water, reflecting every beautiful colour like a lake of mother-of-pearl, made a landscape such as I had never hoped to see save in a picture. The current in the night drifted us twelve miles back, and towards morning we *"let go our anchor, and prayed for"* a steamer.

Thursday, 18th. – Made up our lost way with infinite difficulty, going at the rate of eight knots for five minutes, and then drifting back for ten with the current. We made a triumphant entry into the Dardanelles, in company with the *"Maryanne,"* *"Echinga,"* a man-of-war the name of which we did not know, a French transport, and a steamer. The coast is well wooded and fertile. We saw many Turks assembled on the fort on the lefthand side, and several women, all attracted by the novel sight of so many fine English vessels inside their unknown sea. The current here is so strong that at eight o'clock we cast anchor; and though every eye was strained towards Gallipoli, looking for the steamers, none appeared; and during the night the ship drifted from her moorings, and we were obliged to lower the bower anchor in forty fathoms.

Saturday, 20th. – Yesterday we opened the sealed book of the Dardanelles, and what beauties did it not disclose! – a hilly, rocky coast, with interstices of lovely and fertile valleys clothed in rich green, and shaded with luxuriant trees; forts at every point; some of considerable strength, others more picturesque.

Numbers of cattle and mules were grazing on the shore; and a string of camels, led by a mule with a bell, reminded one more forcibly than anything else, that we were really in the East. Gallipoli, which was visible from a long distance, is a large and apparently a good Turkish town, which means an execrable English one, and is finely situated on a high cliff. It is surrounded by a large English and French encampment.

Gallipoli has now many French and four English regiments stationed there. We hove to for orders, and were immediately despatched to Scutari, for which place we started with the evening breeze, and by eight-o clock we were well into the Sea of Marmora. At three o'clock to-day we caught our first sight of Constantinople, and by nine at night were anchored in the harbour. A Maltese pilot, who came on board at five o'clock, told us that the *"Echinga," "Pride of the Ocean,"* and *"Ganges,"* had arrived a few hours before.

We hear that there are barracks at Scutari capable of holding 6000 men, and that 16,000 can be quartered there by being encamped in the enclosure. Towards sunset we watched the *"Imaum"* ascend the minaret close to us, and presently the town echoed with the call to prayer. Coming to us across the water, the effect was very musical, and somehow it touched me.

Sunday, 21st. – A cold, wet, miserable day, during which we remained at our anchorage. Every one except myself went on shore: Henry tells me that the filth, stenches, and dogs on shore are indescribable. The prospect from the deck is not tempting certainly. The captain returned with news of a steamboat to-morrow to disembark the horses, and also a quay for them to land on. I never was more completely *désillusionée* in my life than with my first day in Constantinople.

Tuesday, 22nd. – Disembarked at last! The tug came alongside very early, and towed us to the quay near Kulali. Such a quay, after our dockyard at Plymouth! – a few old rotten planks, supported on some equally rotten-looking timbers, about three feet above the water's edge. However, they must have been stronger than they looked, for they resisted the plunges and kicks of our horses, as they were tumbled out of the ship, without giving way. No accident befell the disembarkation. Our horses were in wonderfully good condition, and appeared fresh and in good heart. I went ashore, and went up to *"Bob;"* but the sight of him, and the memory of his lost companion, completely upset me, and I could only lay my head on his neck and cry.

A good Greek, who, I suppose, fancied the tears and the horse were someway connected, came and stroked the charger's neck, and said, *"Povero Bobo!"* After dinner, Mr. Philips, Henry, and I rowed up to the barracks in Mr. Coull's gig. They appear from the outside to be a very fine building, close to the sea, and with a very handsome façade; but the inside – the dilapidation! the dirt! the rats! the fleas!!

These last are really so terrible that several officers have been fairly routed by them, and obliged either to pitch their tents on the common, or to sleep on board the ships. No provision whatever has been made for the soldiers; and if Captain Fraser had not put a basket of provisions in the caïque that took the baggage, neither officers nor men would have broken their fast to-night. The stables into which I went first, of course, are more like the crypt of a church than anything else – dark, unpaved, unstalled, of enormous size, and cool: no straw and no mangers!

Wednesday, 24th. – Our orders are to have the ship ready for sea to-morrow, and to re-embark the horses on Friday, to proceed to Varna. We hear that an English frigate has been run on shore by a Greek pilot, and blown up by Russians or Austrians, no one is very clear which. To-day, for the first time since I left England, I induced Mrs. Williams, the sergeant-major's wife, who came out as my maid, to wash a few of the clothes which had accumulated during our voyage. I mention this, as being the first assistance she has ever thought fit to render me since I left England.

Thursday, 25th. – At five this morning a tug came alongside, and took us to the quay at Kulali barracks. Steamers which arrived yesterday evening, confirmed the intelligence respect- the *"Tiger."* We are under orders to proceed to Varna without delay. A more brilliant morning never smiled upon the earth; and I think I never can forget the coup d'œil that presented itself as I ran up on deck. Behind us on either side lay the beautiful city of Constantinople, embowered in trees, and surmounted by its tall and slender minarets. The gay-coloured houses, painted in every imaginable colour, lit up the already brilliant scene; while the picturesque costumes of the Turkish and Greek boatmen, rowing down the current in their gaudy and well-poised caïques, with the long line of Kulali barracks, with its avenue of shady trees, formed a picture of light and shadow truly fascinating. The horse artillery were ranged on the quay, in marching order, with guns mounted, and several pack horses loaded, waiting the signal to embark on their transport, which was moored alongside. Our horses were being exercised beneath the spreading trees. Turkish dogs, lazy and dirty, were lying about in all directions; while horribly filthy beggars were hovering everywhere, interspersed with Turkish soldiers and Greeks. The little harbour is filled with cabbages, and refuse of every description, – a dead dog floating out, and a dead horse drifting close to the shore, on whose swollen and corrupted flanks three dogs were alternately fighting and tearing off the horrible flesh. Beyond this lay the sea, – quiet, blue, serene, and beautiful beyond all words! We hear that our troopers are to return to their stalls in the hold, and that we are to take government horses on our decks. We expected to have to convey an infantry regiment, so we are let off cheaply.

Friday, 26th. – Lord Lucan, who commands the Cavalry, sent an order to Major De Salis, yesterday, to the effect that, *"unless Mrs. Duberly had an order sanctioning her doing so, she was not to re-embark on board the 'Shooting Star,' about to proceed to Varna."* Major De Salis returned for answer, that *"Mrs. Duberly had not disembarked from the 'Shooting Star,' and he had not sufficient authority to order her to do so."*
Up to this time (ten o'clock) I have heard nothing further about it. My dear husband has worried himself into a state of the greatest uneasiness. He looks upon the order as a soldier: I look upon it as a woman, and – laugh at it. Uneasy, of course, I am; as, should the crew refuse to assist me, I must purchase a pony, and ride 130 miles (up to Varna) through a strange and barbarous country, and over the Balkan. Should I find that Lord Lucan has taken other steps to annoy me, I have settled with two of the ship's company, who have agreed to put me on shore and bring me off again after dark, and allow me to remain either on the maindeck or in the hold until we reach Varna; and once landed, and once on horseback, I shall be able to smile at this interference; which is in every way unwarrantable, as I left England by permission of the Horse Guards, and with accommodation provided by the Admiralty. Our horses re-embarked to-day from a temporary quay made of boats and planking. I spent this lovely day imprisoned in my cabin, – thinking it wisest not to appear on deck.

Saturday, 27th. – Major De Salis let me out of durance by telling me that Lord Raglan had been applied to by Lord Lucan, and had stated that he had no intention of interfering with me; so, after luncheon, Henry, Mr. Coull, and I started in Mr. Coull's gig for Pera, and went to Mr. Seager's store, where we met Captain Tomkinson and Dr. Mackay, and all went together to the Stamboul bazaar. What a walk we had!
Alas that the beautiful illusion of this fairy city, as seen from the harbour, should vanish the moment one sets foot in the streets, – paved with small rocks, against which you cut your feet while stumbling over every imaginable abomination! Ownerless dogs lying and prowling about in all directions, – horses and men heavily laden with enormous weights push through the streets, regardless of your shoulders or your toes. The bazaar is certainly worth seeing, but will be too often and too well described to make it necessary for me to enlarge upon it here. It is amusing, if only to listen to the enormous prices asked, and the very small ones taken. I bought some crimson slippers embroidered in gold, and Henry bought a chibouque, and then we all started to walk up to the Hotel de Bellevue for our dinner. The dinner was a failure, though the walk was not; for it was a scramble up a perpendicular hill, repaid with an exquisite view from a graveyard at the top. The row home at night refreshed me both in body and mind.

Sunday, 28th. – Our orders are to be ready to-morrow to sail for Varna. Some one brought a report that, immediately on landing, we were to go three days' march up the country. Nothing is arranged until the last moment; – the authorities do not appear to know their own minds. The subject was discussed at grog-time, and the clamour of opinions and tongues, – some witty, some discontented, some facetious, and some fuddled, – was the most amusing thing possible.

Monday, 29th. – King Charles's day! And never had King Charles more vexations to encounter on that day than we! At half-past seven came the major, with an order that all extra tents, picket poles, &c., should be landed without delay (they having all been embarked the day before). I, not feeling well, remained in bed until ten o'clock. Although the *"Megæra"* steam-ship was ordered to be alongside to tow us at nine this morning, she has not made her appearance, and it is now four. Neither the commanding officers afloat or ashore appear to have the least idea of what they are about. The 17th Lancers have had no order to re-embark; while we, who are only part of a regiment, and without our head-quarters are sent up to encamp at Varna, within sixty miles of the Russian force. Fifteen ponies are purchased to carry the baggage of the regiment; and the allowance for officers is only sufficient to allow Henry and me a bullock-trunk apiece, – rather different to our notions of the *"impedimenta"* of a regiment! They report the commissariat at Varna as being so ill-arranged that we must not expect to get anything but salt meat for some weeks after our arrival.

The *"Megæra"* has just passed us with the 7th Fusileers on board. I waved my hand to Colonel Yea as they passed, the decks crammed with soldiers. I find, by the shaking of the ship that we are weighing anchor, and that the *"Megæra"* is going to take us in tow. The *"Maryanne"* and *"Echinga"* have both passed us on their way up the Bosphorus; – transports are coming up fast alongside Kulali barracks; and, in about an hour, we too shall have looked our last upon the (outwardly) fair city of Stamboul.

Wednesday, 31st. – *"In about an hour!"* Why, we began to weigh anchor at four o'clock on Monday, and at one o'clock to-day it is only just out of the water. Our ship, fitted up in such unseemly haste, has not a rope or a cable on board worth sixpence. The anchor, when half out of the water yesterday, slipped, and the cable breaking disabled two of our best men. Our captain, after running through various courses of rage – swearing and cursing – has become philosophical and smilingly indifferent. Captain Johnson, of the *"Megæra,"* who began at the other end is going rapidly mad. We, the *"Clipper,"* the finest ship afloat, who were the first to receive orders to get under weigh, are the last to leave the harbour. Let me shut up my journal, the subject is too disastrous. Oh, the creaking of that windlass! the convulsive shivering of the ship! the grinding of the hawsers! However, at four o'clock we are off at last; and I think there is not one who does not regret leaving the gay and lovely Bosphorus, and Pera, near which we have been anchored so long, refreshing ourselves with strawberries, oranges, and sherbet, lying lazily on the burning deck, and feeling as though excess of beauty overcame our languid pulses.

Eight o'clock. – We have all been on deck, watching the beauties of the coast as they disappeared behind us: Therapia – where is the Hotel D'Angleterre, the resort of the wives of English naval and military officers, who have *"accompanied their husbands to the seat of war;"* the stone bridge and plane trees of seven stems; the noble viaduct overlooking Beikos Bay, and, finally, the broad surface of the Black Sea. The huge engines and filthy smoke of the *"Megæra"* made our vessel heave and filled us with nausea.

▲ Field Marshal FitzRoy James Henry Somerset, 1st Baron Raglan, born the 30 September 1788 and died the 29 June 1855), known before 1852 as Lord FitzRoy Somerset, was a British Army officer. As a junior officer he served in the Peninsular War and the Hundred Days, latterly as military secretary to the Duke of Wellington. He also took part in politics as Tory Member of Parliament for Truro before becoming Master-General of the Ordnance. He became commander of the British troops sent to the Crimea in 1854: while his primary objective was to defend Constantinople he was ordered to besiege the Russian Port of Sevastopol. After an early success at the Battle of Alma, a failure to deliver orders with sufficient clarity caused the fateful Charge of the Light Brigade at the Battle of Balaclava. Despite further success at the Battle of Inkerman, a piecemeal allied assault on Sevastopol in June 1855 was a complete failure. Somerset died later that month from a mixture of dysentery and clinical depression. Fenton's image.

CHAPTER II

DISEMBARKATION AND ENCAMPMENT AT VARNA

▲ Balaklava harbour by an artwork of William Simpson in 1854 about.

DISEMBARKATION AND ENCAMPMENT AT VARNA

"Quanti valorosi uomini li quali non che altri
ma Galieno, Ippocrate o Esculapio avrieno giudicati sanissimi,
la mattina desinarono co' loro compagni et amici,
che poi la sera vegnente appresso nell' altro mondo
cenarono colli loro passati!"

Boccaccio

ON *Thursday, June* 1st, our disembarkation commenced. We came in sight of Varna about nine o'clock. It is a small but clean-looking town, and certainly, from the harbour, gives one no idea of the impregnable fortress which resisted the Russians in 1828-29. Here the disembarkation of horses was dangerous and awkward, for they were obliged to lower them into boats, and row them ashore. All were frightened – some very restive. One trooper kicked two men, bit a third, and sent a fourth flying overboard. At half past four Henry and I came ashore in Mr. Coull's gig. We took leave of Captain Fraser and the officers of the *"Shooting Star"* with great regret, and, as we rowed off, all hands came aft and cheered. It was kindly and heartily done, and I did not expect it; it overcame me, and filled my eyes with tears. The landing-place gave me a greater realisation of the idea of *"war time"* than any description could do. It was shadowing to twilight.

The quay was crowded with Turks, Greeks, infantry, artillery, and Hussars; piles of cannon balls and shells all around us; rattle of arms everywhere; horses kicking, screaming, plunging; and *"Bob,"* whom I was to ride, was almost unmanageable from excitement and flies. At length, horses were accoutred, and men mounted, and, nearly in the dark, we commenced our march, Henry and I riding first. Luckily, our camp was merely about a mile off. I looked at the streets, vilely paved, full of holes, and as slippery as glass; but feeling how useless was any nervousness, now that the die was cast, I gave the dear old horse his head, and he carried me without a trip to the camp. Out tent had to be brought up with the impedimenta. It was pitch dark, and the dew fell like rain. Major De Salis most kindly came to meet me, and, taking me to his tent, gave me some ham, biscuit, and brandy and water, and allowed me to lie down until my own tent was erected.

Friday, 2nd. – A broiling day. There is no tree or shelter of any sort near our encampment, which is finely situated on a large plain fronting the lake. Artillery, Turkish cavalry, and eight regiments of infantry compose our camp at present, though, through the dust on my right hand, I can discern French troops marching in fast. Some of our infantry tents are pitched on mounds, which mounds are the graves of those Russians who fell in the campaign of 1828-29.

Saturday, 3rd. – About ten o'clock Major De Salis brought us some milk in a bottle, and we broiled a slice of the ham kindly given us by Captain Fraser, of the *"Shooting Star,"* and so, over the camp fire, we made our breakfast. Our dinner at night consisted of the same, as no other rations than bread have been served out; and but for our ham we should have had no meat at all. Later, a welcome sight presented itself in the shape of Captain Fraser and some bottles of beer, one of which I drank like a thirsty horse. The horses are wild with heat and flies, and they scream and kick all day and night. Lord Cardigan and staff rode into our lines. Henry went into Varna, and bought a very fine grey cob pony, of the British consul, for twenty guineas. Captain Eden, of the *"London,"* called on me and invited me to church and luncheon to-morrow. Captain Tomkinson, Mr. Philips, Dr. Mackay, Henry, and I dine on board the "Shooting Star." Am I not hungry?

Sunday, 4th. – We started on horseback at half-past nine to meet the *"gig,"* which was waiting for us in the harbour. Lady Erroll, whom I am curious to see, was also asked, but as Lord Erroll was detained in camp she could not leave. After service we inspected the ship, a magnificent two-decker of ninety guns, and partook of a most refreshing luncheon. Lord George Paulet, who had written to me in the morning, came and carried us off to the *"Bellerophon,"* and entertained us most hospitably. When we rode home at night, we found the 17th Lancers disembarking. Captain Wallace, 7th Fusileers, who was killed yesterday by a fall from his pony, was buried to-day – the first-fruits of the sacrifice! We march to-morrow morning at five to Devna, a village about nineteen miles up the country. After I had packed, I sat down outside the tent, and wrapped myself in the novel beauties of the scene – the great plain bordered by the vast lake; the glorious colours of sunset; the warlike confusion of foreground; hussar and artillery horses picketed; infantry encamped; Turkish soldiers galloping here and there on their active little horses; Bashi-Basouks all round us, and the smoke of the camp-fires throwing a blue haze over the whole.

Monday, 5th. – Was awoke by the *reveillée* at half-past two; rose, packed our bedding and tent, got a stale egg and a mouthful of brandy, and was in my saddle by half-past five. I never shall forget that march! It occupied nearly eight hours. The heat intense, the fatigue overwhelming; but the country – anything more beautiful I never saw! – vast plains; verdant hills, covered with shrubs and flowers; a noble lake; and a road, which was merely a cart track, winding through a luxuriant woodland country, across plains and through deep bosquets of brushwood. A most refreshing river runs near our camp, but we have no trees, no shelter.
Captain Tomkinson made me a bed of his cloak and sheepskin; and drawing my hat over my eyes, I lay down under a bush, close to *"Bob,"* and slept till far towards evening.

Tuesday, 6th. – The major was busy in arranging and settling the men; but towards the afternoon, Captain Tomkinson, Henry, and I rode into the village, to try to procure some vin du pays for our dinner (wherein we failed); and to the hills, to try for some green forage for our horses, as the straw brought us by the natives is little else than old bed stuffing, and full of fleas. We met one of the commanders of the Turkish army going with an escort to Schumla. His belt and holsters were most magnificently chased. He was on the small horse of the country, and had just mounted a fresh relay. His escort looked like a collection of beggars on horseback; but the little active horses sprang into a gallop at once, and kept it up over tracks that would puzzle many a clever English hunter. After our horses had fed on long grass and flowers, we came home to our dinner.
A French colonel in the Turkish service, Colonel Du Puy, called on us in the evening, and interested us much by his account of his last winter's campaigning in this comfortless country.

Wednesday, 7th. – Captain Tomkinson and Mr. Clutterbuck, each with eight men, went out to patrol: they went about ten miles, in different directions, but saw no Cossacks. Lord Cardigan joined this detachment of the brigade to-day. Part of the 17th Lancers also marched in.

Saturday, 10th. – The head quarters and Captain Lockwood's troop have arrived at Varna, and were expected up to-day; but as they had no baggage ponies, nor any means of conveyance for the baggage, they were detained until we could send down our ponies to bring them up. This does not strike me as being well arranged. Whose fault is it? The infantry of the Light Division were also ordered up to Devna to-day, to form a large camp in conjunction with us; but as it poured with rain they could not march. Captain Tomkinson, with a sergeant and nine men, has been away on patrol these three days, but is expected back to-night. Lord Cardigan forbids them to take their cloaks to wrap round them at night, as he considers it *"effeminate."*
Luckily it is summer, though the dews fall like rain. Our camp is most picturesque, in the midst of a large and fertile plain, near a sparkling river, and carpetted with brilliant flowers – burrage, roses, larkspurs, heather, and a lovely flower the name of which I do not know. Henry and I wandered among the hills this afternoon; and Bob sped over the long grass and delicate convolvuli, neighing with delight at being loosed from his picket rope, where he has been rained and blown upon incessantly for two days and nights.

Monday, 12th. – Captain Tomkinson returned to-day from Basardchick, bringing me a handful of roses from the ruined village, observing, as he gave them to me, that I now possessed roses from nearer the enemy than any one else.

Thursday, 15th. – A mail came up to-day, brought up by an orderly from Varna. I received letters from S., F., and E. I also got a Devizes' paper, which pleased me much. The morning wet and chilly; the noon hot and sultry.

Friday, 16th. – A report was rife in camp that 57,000 Austrians were marching to our assistance against the Russians; also that the whole force, English and French, will be under immediate marching orders for Silistria, as 90,000 Russians are investing the town.

Saturday, 17th. – Weather intensely hot – no shade, no breeze. Head quarters marched up to-day from Varna. Mr. Philips left to-day for Tirnova, where he was sent to purchase 500 horses. They inform us to-day that the Austrian force is 300,000, and it is uncertain upon which side they will fight. What a comfort we find in our double marquee tent! The lining excludes the heat more effectually than anything else, and it is so much more easy of ventilation than a bell tent. The Bulgarian pony *"Whisker,"* proving too active with his heels, was obliged to be picketted by himself, and not liking it, amused himself, and bothered us, by untying the knot with his teeth, and scampering all over the country. The Light Division are really expected up on Monday, when it is supposed we shall begin our march in earnest. Such an expectation fills all minds with excitement and hope: I pity the Russian army which encounters our men as they are now. We hear wonders of the valour of the Turks. Every day the Russians make breaches in the walls, and rushing on to the attack, are beaten off every day by these dauntless men at the point of the bayonet. The Russians, a few days since, sent in a flag of truce to bury their dead: the Turks not only agreed, but sent a party to assist.

Wednesday, 21st. – The 5th Dragoon Guards and two troops of the 13th Light Dragoons marched to join our encampment to-day. The former took up a position nearer the river, but the 13th came up on our right, between the 17th Lancers and ourselves. Yesterday we performed a *"grand march:"* we shifted our ground, and went about 200 yards further up the valley. This movement occupied us from six, A.M., to three, P.M. The ground, which had not been previously marked out, took some time to choose, and Lord Cardigan and *aides-de-camp* were a wearisome time in arranging it; and when it was arranged, we were put more than a mile from the water; whereas, by a different disposition of the troops, all might have been equally near to the river bank.

▲ *French army landing in Varna.*

Thursday, 22nd. – Henry and I started at half-past twelve to ride over to the Infantry camp; Captain Lockwood mounted me on his roan horse, and Henry rode the grey. We missed our track, and made thirteen miles out of seven. We wandered through most exquisite woodlands, through sunny glades and banks of sweet spring flowers, passed trees through whose green leaves the golden sunlight fell dropping in a shower, and through deep shadows and thickets, beneath which our horses could hardly force their way. Arrived at the camp, we inquired for about a dozen of our friends, and found they had every one, without a single exception, *"gone into Varna;"* so there was nothing for it but to turn our horses' heads homewards through the weary heat. Hurrying home to be in time for dinner (we had had nothing but a piece of bread and a glass of water, kindly given me by a good commissary), we found only disappointment for the bottom of the pot had come out, and all the stew was in the fire.

Friday, 23rd. – The 17th Lancers got up some pony races to-day, over a tolerable course of a mile. Captain Morgan won gallantly, on a pony for which he had paid 50s.

Sunday, 25th. – Was awoke at four o'clock from a profound sleep, by the words, *"A general order for the regiment to be prepared as soon as possible to march thirty miles."* All the camp was alive No tents were to be struck, but every one was to move. We could make nothing of the order, until we heard that a courier had arrived to say that the Russians had abandoned the siege of Silistria, and had crossed the Danube.

We still dressed in hot haste, wondering at the order, when an *aide-de-camp* came up to say that only a squadron of the 8th and a squadron of the 13th were to go; and that they were to march towards Silistria to make a reconnaissance of the Russian army. The order to *"bridle and saddle"* was given, and all was ready for a start, when a counter-order arrived – *"The squadrons are to wait until three days' provisions are cooked;"* so that of the whole regiment roused at four, two troops went away at half-past ten. If it takes six hours and a half to get two squadrons under weigh, how long will it take to move the whole British force? At six o'clock Henry, Major de Salis, and I rode over to the Turkish camp to dine with Colonel Du Puy. We met Mr. G—, the correspondent of the Daily News, also M. Henri, and another officer, *aides-de-camp* to Maréchal St. Arnaud.

These two last were returning from Schumla, whither they had conveyed a fine Turkish horse, as a gift from the Maréchal to Omar Pasha. I saw the little horse. He was about fourteen hands, black, with the exception of two white marks and a white foot. Omar Pasha returned him, as a Turkish superstition prevents the soldiers from riding horses not entirely of a colour. He who rides a black, bay, or chestnut horse with white marks, or a white foot behind, will assuredly be slain in battle. A Turkish officer joined our party during the evening; and after sitting for some time in silence, smoking his chibouque, he informed me, through his interpreter (he had been staring at me for half an hour previously) that it was only permitted him to sit in my presence during war-time; under any other circumstances he could not sit down with a woman who was unveiled.

Monday, 26th. – Henry rode into Varna to procure money from the commissariat chest. I went out to meet him in the afternoon, and Captain Chetwode rode with me. We went as far as the Infantry camp at Aladyn, and on our way passed the head-quarters of the 13th, marching up to join our camp. The lovely evening and clear sky induced us to prolong our ride so far, and we found Henry among the officers of the 23rd Welsh Fusiliers, who most hospitably pressed us to stay and partake of their excellent dinner, which we did. On our way home, in the almost impenetrable twilight, we passed close by Captain Tomkinson's poor horse, which fell under him last night as he was returning from Varna. There he lay stark and stiff, a white mass amid the dark shadows – as fine a fencer as ever strained upon the bit on a hunting morning; and, hark! the gallop and baying of the wild dogs, even now trooping over the hills to feed upon his almost palpitating heart! Ah! mournful sight, that he should lie there, so ghastly and so still!

Thursday, 29th. – Two troops of the 11th Hussars joined us to-day. We had no news of Lord Cardigan's patrol until after dinner, when Bowen rode into the lines on Captain Lockwood's roan horse, who bore him feebly to the picket ropes, and then fell down. For many minutes he appeared dying of exhaustion, but eventually we revived him with brandy and water. Bowen tells us that the squadrons will not return for some days; that their fatigue has been excessive, and their hardships very great. They appear to have been marching incessantly, for which hard work neither men nor horses are fit. A French colonel on his way to Silistria dined with us this afternoon, and interested us much by his accounts of the Turkish army. He told us no army cost so much to maintain, with such infamous results. The soldiers are neither fed nor clothed. All the money which passes through the hands of the pashas sticks to their fingers. Often, when halting after a long march, they inquire whether any meat is to be served out to them. *"No!"* *"Any bread?"* *"No!"* They shrug their shoulders and betake themselves to cold water and a pipe. A more wretched appearance than that which they present cannot be imagined; but at Silistria they have proved their courage.

Friday, 30th. – Part of the Light Division marched up this morning, and encamped on the opposite side of the valley. The Rifles marched in first; next followed the 33rd, playing *"Cheer, boys, cheer;"* and cheerily enough the music sounded across our silent valley, helping many a *"willing, strong right hand,"* ready to faint with heat and fatigue. The 88th Connaught Rangers gave a wild Irish screech (I know no better word) as they saw their fellow countrymen, the 8th Royal Irish Hussars, and they played *"Garry Owen"* with all their might; while the 77th followed with *"The British Grenadier."* A troop of R. H. A. also came up to Devna. The accession of 7,000 men will be like a plague of locusts: they will eat up our substance. We can get little else but stale eggs, tough chickens, and sour milk, and now we shall not get even that; and the cries of *"Yak-mak Johnny!"* *"Sud Johnny!"* *"Eur mooytath Johnny!"* will be transferred from the cavalry to the *"opposition lines."*

Sunday, July 2nd. – Captain Tomkinson returned to-day from Silistria, whither he had been sent to ascertain the best road for marching troops. He described the whole Russian force. although they have lately raised the siege of Silistria, as being still in sight of the town, and speaks much of their numerous field pieces.
He brought back a Russian round shot, and told me he had seen two of the enemy, but lying cold and still.
I hear the Turks are hardly to be restrained from mutilating their dead foes. If they can do so unseen, they will cut off three or four heads, and, stringing them together through the lips and cheeks, carry them over their shoulders, like a rope of onions. The Turks inform us that the Russians say they will treat the Turks whom they make prisoners, as prisoners of war, but the French and English will be treated as felons, and sent to Siberia; and really, if the Russians are as uncleanly, smell as strong, and eat as much garlic as the Turks, it will be the best thing that can happen to us under the circumstances We have had a hurricane all day, filling our tents, eyes, dinners, hair, beds, and boxes with intolerable dust. Our chicken for dinner was so tough that not even our daily onions could get it down. We were forced to shake our heads at our plates, and relinquish the dinner. The black bread, which is kneaded on the ground, is a happy mixture of sand, ants, and barley – and it is besides so sour that it makes my eyes water.

Monday, 3rd. – At three o'clock we were ordered to turn out as quickly as possible in light marching order, to receive Omar Pasha, who wished to inspect the troops, and was on his road from Schumla to Varna, where he was to hold a council of war. In ten minutes the cavalry were mounted, and Henry and I started upon Bob and the Great Grey, to see the man whom war had made so famous. His appearance struck me as military and dignified. He complimented all our troops, and insisted on heading the Light Cavalry charge, which made me laugh, for he was on a small Turkish horse, and had to scramble, with the spurs well in, to get out of the way of our long striding English horses. He was loudly cheered; appeared highly gratified; made me a bow and paid me a compliment, and proceeded to his carriage to continue his journey.

Thursday, 6th. – Reports of a more peaceful nature reach us. We hear that Omar Pasha is the only counsellor for war. The Russian force is retreating daily. Now the *"shave"* is, that Austria is beginning to be afraid lest the English and French armies should decline to leave this fertile land, and all the powers, inimical or neutral, appear desirous to hush the matter up. The party which returned to-day from Silistria inform us of the good feeling shown by the Turks to their Russian prisoners. They feed them with their meat and rice, and treat them with every mark of kindness and consideration. The peaceful reports which reach us give dissatisfaction.
We are all for one good fight, to see which is the better man: all for one blow, struck so effectually as to crush all warlike propensities against us for ever. We hear to-day of the terrible fate of the *"Europa."* Report at present speaks so vaguely that we know not what to believe. At first we were told that every soul had perished, and afterwards that only Colonel Willoughby Moore and the veterinary surgeon fell victims to

this terrible catastrophe. A more frightful tragedy could scarcely occur than the burning of a transport ship – soldiers ignorant of seafaring, and horses crammed in the hold! Omar Pasha returned again to-day, and on his way inspected the Heavy Cavalry and Artillery. Lord Raglan also came up, and the staff made a brilliant-display. Omar Pasha again expressed himself in the most complimentary manner; and after it was all over, Henry and I turned our horses' heads and went for a ride.

Tuesday, 11th. – The reconnaissance, under Lord Cardigan, came in this morning at eight, having marched all night. They have been to Rassova, seen the Russian force, lived for five days on water and salt pork; have shot five horses, which dropped from exhaustion on the road, brought back an araba full of disabled men, and seventy-five horses, which will be, as Mr. Grey says, unfit for work for many months, and some of them will never work again. I was out riding in the evening when the stragglers came in; and a piteous sight it was – men on foot, driving and goading on their wretched, wretched horses, three or four of which could hardly stir. There seems to have been much unnecessary suffering, a cruel parade of death, more pain inflicted than good derived; but I suppose these sad sights are merely the casualties of war, and we must bear them with what courage and fortitude we may. One of these unfortunate horses was lucky enough to have his leg broken by a kick, as soon as he came in, and was shot. There is an order that no horse is to be destroyed unless for glanders or a broken leg.

Thursday, 13th. – A long morning was spent in investigating the state of the horses by Colonel Shewell, Lord Cardigan, and Mr. Grey. I despatched letters to Captain Fraser, of the *"Shooting Star,"* and Lady Duberly.
A sad event closed this day. One of our sergeants, who had been ill for some days previously, left the hospital tent about three o'clock, A.M., and when our watering parade went down to the river, they found his body in the stream: he was quite dead. He was a steady and most respectable man: could he have had a foreboding of the lingering deaths of so many of his comrades, and so rashly have chosen his own time to appear before God? The band of the Connaught Rangers came at seven o'clock to play him to a quieter resting-place than the bed of the sparkling, babbling stream – a solitary grave dug just in front of our lines, and near enough for us, during our stay, to protect him from the dogs. Three more of the reconnoitring party's horses are lying in the shadow of death. I had been pained by all this, and Henry and I, ordering our horses, rode out, in the cloudless summer evening, to a quiet little village nestled among the hills, where the storks build their nests on the old tree-tops that shade the trickling fountain where the cattle drink.
Colonel Shewell met us as we rode into camp with a radiant face, telling us that all the transports are ordered up from Varna, and that we are to embark immediately for Vienna, as the Russians are so enraged with Austria for taking part against us that they have determined on besieging that place.

Saturday, 15th. – The Vienna *"shave"* turned out false; instead, came an order desiring that all our heavy baggage should be sent to Varna, to be forwarded to Scutari. Heavy baggage! when we are already stript of everything but absolute necessaries, and are allowed barely sufficient ponies to transport what we have!
Letters arrived last night, but were not delivered till to-day. Yesterday evening Henry and I took a lovely ride to Kosludsche, a small town about eight miles from the camp. The pastoral scenes, in this land of herds and flocks, speak in flute-like tones of serenity and repose – the calm, unruffled lives of the simple people, the absence of all excitement, emulation, traffic, or noise; valley and hill-side sending home each night its lowing herds, and strings of horses, flocks of sheep and goats. The lives of the inhabitants are little removed above the cattle which they tend; but to one who *"has forgotten more life than most people ever knew,"* the absence of turmoil and all the *"stale and unprofitable uses of the world,"* the calm aspect of the steadfast hills, the quietude of the plains, and the still small voices of the flowers, all tell me, that however worn the mind may be, however bruised the heart, nature is a consoler still; and we who have fretted away our lives in vain effort and vainer show, find her large heart still open to us, and in the shadow of the eternal hills a repose for which earth has no name.

Sunday, 16th. – Henry and I took a new ride this evening. We turned into the gorge to the left of our camp; but leaving the araba track, we struck into a narrow footpath, embowered with trees, and frowned over by stern and perpendicular rocks, at whose foot ran the narrow fissure along which we rode slowly.

Emerging at last, we came on an open plain covered with heavy crops of barley; crossing this for a short distance, we came presently into another thick copse of underwood, down which we had to ride, over precipitous and rocky ground, where the horses could barely keep their footing, and where a false step must have been fatal. The stars lighted our track, and we descended safely. We found ourselves on the road to Devna, and, waking up our horses, we cantered over the plain to our camp.

Wednesday, 19th. – I have mentioned nothing that has happened since Sunday; as, except the usual routine of parades and camp-life, and perpetual fresh reports as to our eventual destination, nothing has occurred. But to-day we lost one of the poor fellows who had returned ill from the reconnoitring expedition. He came back with low fever, and, after being two days insensible, expired this afternoon. Henry and I, accompanied by Captains Hall Dare and Evans of the 23rd, rode to-day to Pravadi. We started at one o'clock, and returned soon after eight. Next to Silistria, Pravadi is the strongest fortified town in Bulgaria. The town lies in what (approaching from the Devna side) appears to be an abyss. High, perpendicular rocks, like the boundaries of a stern sea-coast, enclose it, east and west. Fortifications protect it on the south, and a fortification and broad lake on the north. We rode to it through lovely home scenery, softened by the blue range of the Balkan in the distance. We saw almost to Varna. In the town we found shops, and purchased damson-cheese and some Turkish scarfs. My pony, *"Whisker,"* cast a shoe in going, and Captain Hall Dare started without one; so we stopped at a farrier's and had them shod. My saddle excited immense curiosity. They touched and examined it all over; and several men tried to sit in it, but Henry prevented them. We went to a café, where we got a cup of first-rate coffee; and at about half-past four, we started to ride home. Oh, the heat! We made a ride of about twenty-two miles, but its beauty well repaid us for our trouble. The Turks have a unique way of shoeing horses. One man fastens a cord round the horse's fetlock, and so holds up his leg; a second man holds aside the animal's tail, and with a horse-hair flapper keeps away the flies; a third man holds his head and talks to him; while the fourth, squatting on the ground, with his head on a level with the horse's foot, hammers away with all his might at eight nails, four on each side.

Friday, 21st. – News came that Sir G. Brown had gone to the Crimea, to discover the best place for landing troops, and that we should follow him before long – at which we were glad.

Sunday, 23rd. – The cholera is come amongst us! It is not in our camp, but is in that of the Light Division, and sixteen men have died of it this day in the Rifles. We hear the whole camp is to be broken up; the Light Division are to march to Monastir, and we are under orders to march to Issyteppe to-morrow. I regret this move very much, as it will separate me from Lady Erroll, whose acquaintance has been the greatest comfort and pleasure to me; but I trust we shall soon be quartered together again, as no one but myself can tell the advantage I have derived from the friendship of such a woman.

Monday, 24th. – The march is postponed, owing to the difficulty of finding sufficient water at Jeni-bazaar, which is to be our destination. Captain Lockwood volunteered to ascertain for Lord Cardigan what were the supplies of water, and started for that purpose this afternoon. I, acting on Lady Erroll's suggestion, rode down to the 11th lines this evening to call on Mrs. Cresswell, who has arrived with her husband, Captain Cresswell, of the 11th Hussars. I could not but pity the unnecessary discomforts in which the poor lady was living, and congratulated myself and Henry, as we rode away, on our pretty marquee and green bower.
Present orders say we do not march till Wednesday. Lord Cardigan has been searching unsuccessfully for another camping-ground. Mr. Macnaghten, who rode into Varna, tells me that the transports are all being ordered up, but that the *"Shooting Star"* had been cast on account of defective rigging.
Henry rode into Varna. Towards evening I started on horseback with Captain Chetwode to meet him, and we rode to Aladyn. The infantry of our division moved to-day eight miles over the hills. They move, in the hope of averting that fearful malady which has crept among them. We hear it is raging at Varna, and that a quarantine is established between that place and Constantinople. For ourselves, we have had a solitary case of small-pox; but the poor fellow has been taken to the hospital at Varna to-day.

Tuesday, 25th. – Orders to march to-morrow morning to Issyteppe.

Two o'clock, P.M. – Captain Lockwood having returned, and reported an insufficiency of water, he was ordered to repair again to the place to endeavour to discover water in the neighbourhood.

Three o'clock. – March postponed till to-morrow night at soonest, Lord Cardigan having taken a fancy to a night march. There is no moon just now.

Five o'clock. – March definitely settled for to-morrow morning at six.

Thursday, 27th. – The cavalry of the Light Division, with Captain Maude's troop of Horse Artillery, marched this morning to Issyteppe, – a wretched village, situated in a large plain about twelve miles from Devna.
A most uninteresting country led to it, – flat and bare, destitute of trees or water, except one half-dried fountain, with a rotting carcass lying beside it. When we attempted to water our thirsty horses, only few could drink; the rest had to hold on, as best they could, till they reached their journey's end. A now dry, boggy ditch, which runs through the village, brought a plague of frogs to our camp; and a heavy thunderstorm, rattling on our heads as we sat on the sward at dinner, drove us, drenched and uncomfortable, to our tents, and wetted our boxes. Captain Lockwood and I walked down to the village before sunset, to endeavour to procure an araba wheel (ours had come off), also a chicken for to-morrow's breakfast; but we failed in both: there was nothing but old women, cats, and onions in the place.

Friday, 28th. – My husband's birthday! and he is likely to be, for to-day at least, miserable enough.
We were roused, wet and dreary, at three o'clock. At six we were in our saddles; and a very distressing march I found it, though it did not exceed fourteen miles. The heat was intolerable, the sun blinding.
The horses again started without water, nor was there any between Issyteppe and Jeni-bazaar. We reached the latter place about half-past eleven; and immediately after the piquet poles were put down, there was a simultaneous rush to the fountains of the town to water the horses. Poor wretches, how they rushed to the water! Poor old Hatchet (Captain Lockwood's horse) nearly went head foremost down the well, while others upset bucket after bucket, by thrusting their heads into them before they reached the ground.
There was a fine group of trees near a fountain opposite our lines, and under their refreshing shade the brigadier pitched his tent. A feeling of great dissatisfaction was caused by the troops being forbidden either to water their horses, or to obtain water for the use of the officers, from the fountain in question, although the other fountains are so far off. The fountain, being so little drained, overflowed in the night, and a fatigue party were put in requisition to make a drain. If Æsop were alive, I wonder if this would inspire him with another fable? To-night I am thoroughly exhausted with fatigue.

Sunday, 30th. – Lord Cardigan tells us to-day that we shall remain here until we go into winter quarters at Adrianople.

Tuesday, August 1st. – Our tents not being pitched on the right (our place as senior regiment out), Lord Cardigan changed us to-day, causing us to change places with the 13th Light Dragoons.
Our tents when changed were not quite in a line, though I confess it was barely perceptible; but at evening we had to strike and move all our tents about a foot and a half further back. We hear to-day that the Light Division have lost 100 men and 4 officers.

Friday, 4th. – I regret to say that poor Captain Levinge, of the R. H. A., is dead. The report is, that having been suffering from incipient cholera, he took an over-dose of laudanum. He is much regretted. An artilleryman of Captain Maude's troop died of cholera, and was buried yesterday. This is our first case of cholera.
Captain Stevenson, 17th Lancers, took me for a ride this evening to a wondrous gorge, about three miles from our camp. We passed suddenly from a sunny landscape, laden with grain, into Arabia Petræa.
It was as though the hills had been rifted asunder, so high, narrow, sombre, and stern were the gloomy walls that almost threatened to close over our heads. A small torrent ran at the foot, tumbling over huge masses of rock, which had fallen from the grim heights above. I felt oppressed; and reaching the open fields once more, put Bob into a canter, which he seemed as willing to enjoy as myself.

Saturday, 5th. – *"I never watched upon a wilder night."* At evening-tide it was hot and sultry, but at midnight up came the wind, sweeping broadly and grandly over the plain. We feared for our tent, although well secured; and presently across the hurricane came booming the great guns of the thunder.

The lightning seemed to pierce our eyelids. By morning every trace of storm had vanished, and day looked out smiling as before, though her lashes were gemmed with heavy tear-drops, and the deep trees near us at intervals shivered out a sigh. The adjutant-general came to camp to-day. He says the Infantry are under orders to embark on the 16th for the Crimea. Are we to go too? or are we to be left out here, to constitute a travelling Phœnix Park for Lord . . . ?

Thursday, 10th. – Rose at half-past three, and by five, Henry, Captain Tomkinson, Captain Chetwode, Mr. Mussenden, and I were starting for Schumla. We broke into a canter after leaving the village of Jeni-bazaar, and in two hours and five minutes reached Schumla, a distance of fifteen miles. Here we met Captain Saltmarshe, Mr. Trevelyan, and Mr. Palmer, of the 11th, and Mr. Learmouth of the 17th, and had a joint breakfast, and a very nasty one, at the Locanda, kept by Hungarians. That over, we walked about the town.

It is very picturesque; the houses are nestled in trees, but are irregular, dirty, and mean. In the Greek shops we succeeded in making a few purchases, such as a glass tumbler, five-china plates, a soup ladle (tin), and some Turkish towels. I tried hard to procure some tea, lemons, or arrowroot for our sick in hospital, but I might as well have asked for a new-fashioned French bonnet. They did not know what I wanted.

I bought a fine Turkish bridle, and we returned to the Locanda, where I lay down on the boards (Oh, how hard they were!) to try to sleep for an hour. It was impossible. The bugs took a lease of me, and the fleas, in innumerable hosts, disputed possession. A bright-eyed little mouse sat demurely in the corner watching me, and twinkling his little black eyes as I stormed at my foes. Our dinner was tough meat and excellent champagne, which we did not spare; and after admiring the sunset tints on the fine forts of the town, we again got into our saddles; and a great moon, with a face as broad, red, round, and honest as a milkmaid's, shed her hearty beams over us and lighted us home, and afterwards to bed. Poor Major Willett lies sick in the village of Jeni-bazaar, where he has been moved for the sake of quiet.

Friday, 11th. – Ilinsky (or some such name), the Hungarian commandant, came over and dined with us. Two or three funerals to-day. The 5th Dragoon Guards are suffering terribly from cholera. Two days ago eleven men died. The report of the great fire in Varna, which reached us two days since, proves to be quite correct. It seems to have ravaged the town. Various rumours are afloat concerning its origin; some suppose it was set on fire by the Greeks, at Russian instigation. Many shops, and much of the commissariat stores, are burnt; and the plunder during the fire was said to be enormous. Our supplies must in future be drawn from Schumla. Why has there been no branch commissariat at Schumla? Varna is a two-days' march from us. It is also a fact, that the commissariat chest in Varna was guarded by one slovenly Turkish sentry. Our sad sickness increases. Our hospital tents are full. Poor Mr. Philips is now attacked with fever; and the sun sets daily on many new-made graves. A second hospital marquee arrived for our regiment to-day.

Wednesday, 16th. – To-day's mail brought us the sad news of the death of Miss D., Henry's step-sister, – loved and regretted by us all. This took away the pleasure we felt in the arrival of our letters.

Thursday, 17th. – Henry and I took a long ride, to endeavour to shake off the depression which this perpetual sickness forces upon one. We had never before seen suffering that we could not alleviate; but here there are no comforts but scanty medical stores, and the burning, blistering sun glares upon heads already delirious with fever. I am sure that nervous apprehension has much to do with illness; and, indeed, if the mind abandons itself to the actual contemplation of our position, it is enough to make it quail.

Friday, 18th. – Poor Mrs. Blaydes (my servant), after recovering from an attack of fever, brought on a relapse to-day from over-anxiety to attend to my comforts. She endeavoured to work till her health absolutely forbad it; and a great assistance she was to me. Poor woman! she has been insensible since morning. A woman of the 13th died to-day. Hospital marquees were shifted to fresh ground, as it was observed that men put into them almost invariably died. Henry and I rode to where Captain Chetwode and Mr. Clutterbuck were shooting;

and on our return we met Lord Cardigan, who tells me all the talk is of Sebastopol; and he thinks the Light Cavalry will be under orders before long. Another mail, laden with heavy news. Poor little W.! F.'s only son! I have so many feelings in my heart; and yet they must all be absorbed in sympathy for the sorrowing father and mourning mother!

Saturday, 10th. – Rode with Henry to a village on the left of our camp, about six miles off, the name of which I do not know. What a ride that was!

"What a day it was that day! Hills and vales did openly Seem to heave and throb away At the sight of the great sky; And the silence, as it stood In the glory's golden flood, Audibly did bud and bud."

After climbing up the sides of an interminable hill, we reached the table land – oaks, walnuts, filberts, a very wilderness of trees! We plunged down into a deep and leafy gorge, stopped at the wayside fountain, and finally emerged into the broad plain of the camp. Sunday, 20th. – Poor Mrs. Blaydes expired this morning! Truly, we are in God's hands, and far enough from the help of man! Insufficient medical attendance (many of the doctors are ill), scanty stores, and no sick diet – we must feed our dying on rations and rum!

As far as I am concerned, I feel calm, and filled with a tranquil faith: I have the strongest trust in the wise providence of God. Monday, 21st – Went out with Henry over the stubble to shoot quail; Captain Chetwode had the gun, and killed several brace.

Tuesday, 22nd. – Henry made a *"salmi"* of the quail for breakfast that was truly delicious: I could be a gourmet, if I could always feed on such salmis. Mr. Clowes, Henry, and I went out to-day; Henry shooting, Mr. Clowes and I beating from our ponies with long whips.

Wednesday, 23rd. – Mr. Maxse, aide-de-camp to Lord Cardigan, who has returned to-day from Varna (sick-leave), says the troops are embarking fast; that the harbour is filled with transports; that siege guns are being put on board, and every preparation making for an expedition to the Crimea. We are reanimated!

The sickness decreases; cooler weather is coming on; things look more cheerily now. We rode to-day with Captain Tomkinson – such a pretty ride! Going south for five miles, we turned to our right on smooth, long turf, by a little stream whose course was only marked by the flowers along its banks. Then came large trees bowed down with foliage, and hill sides matted with creeping plants, clematis and vine. Turning homeward, we saw fields of tobacco and Indian corn. We were a long way from home; so waking up our ponies, we left the Turkish camp and conical hill on our left, and galloped over the turf to Jeni-bazaar, and then up-hill to our lines.

Thursday, 24th. – Returning from a ride among the filbert trees – how the nuts fell into our hands and laps! – we met Mr. Maxse riding at a gallop. He bore orders for our immediate embarkation at Varna for Sebastopol. The artillery and 11th Hussars are to march to-morrow; we, and the 13th and 17th, follow on Saturday.

The order was heard silently; not a single cheer: we have waited in inaction too long. Sickness and death are uppermost in our thoughts just now. I also am not well – the hard food tells on me; and to become well, rest and change of diet are necessary: but I don't see much chance of getting either.

Saturday, 26th. – We started at ten o'clock on our first day's march. We left our poor colonel on the ground, too ill to be moved. Mr. Philips and Mr. Somers were also left behind in the village, to follow as they best could. We halted at Issyteppe, where we had also stopped on our way up. Here the 13th and 17th remained until Monday; and we fondly hoped to do the same, but are ordered to march on to-morrow to Gottuby.

Both our servants, Connell and Hopkins, are ill; and I am very suffering, so much so as to doubt my ability to march to-morrow.

Sunday, 27th. – Marched to Gottuby, and encamped on the cholera-stricken ground just vacated by the Heavies. We had appalling evidence of their deaths! Here and there a heap of loose earth, with a protruding hand or foot, showed where the inhabitants had desecrated the dead, and dug them up to possess themselves of the blankets in which they were buried. Nevertheless, we gladly halted, for the heat was very distressing; though it would have been better if the sick had gone on to Devna, as they will now have no halt in their march to-morrow. The 13th who remained at Issyteppe, lost a man of cholera. He was taken ill at four, and buried at six o'clock. We do not start before nine o'clock to-morrow. I hope to be able to ride.

Monday, 28th. – A cold, showery morning refreshed us all, and made the horses' coats stare. Oh, how much have I, though only slightly ill, felt the miseries attendant on sickness out here! It depresses one to know that every remedy is out of one's power. Come rain, come heat, on you must go: were it not for my trust in the Great Strength my heart would fail. We reached Devna about eleven, glad to see the old place again.

And the river! how we walked the horses up and down in it, and how they thrust their parched heads into the stream, than which no stream ever seemed so limpid or so sweet!

Tuesday, 29th. – *"March at half-past six to Varna."* March delayed till half-past seven, at which time we started (I with an æther bottle) over the hills to Aladyn, and so to Varna by the upper road.

The colonel was unable to leave his bed, and followed in an araba. The ride was beautiful. We passed a singular geological formation of large rocks, resembling the ruins of a huge temple with many towers.

We reached our camping ground (the middle of a stubble field) at twelve o'clock. We passed two camps on the road – one Sir De L. Evans's; the other a part of the Light Division, consisting of the 19th, 77th, and 88th. The 88th seemed in sad spirits: they lost their surgeon yesterday of cholera, and the major was then supposed to be dying. All round us are camped the various regiments – French and English Cavalry, Infantry, and Artillery, and Turkish Infantry and Cavalry. The Rifles embarked to-day. I heard that Lady Erroll was seen riding into Varna, to embark with them. Colonel Yea (7th Fusiliers) called on me, and told me that his regiment was to embark to-morrow in the *"Emperor;"* he also said his regiment was to be the first to land.

At five o'clock we saw no chance of getting anything to eat (we had had nothing since six in the morning), and I could not bear it any longer; so we saddled the ponies, and cantered into Varna.

Here of course we found all the shops closed, but at length discovered a small restaurateur in a back street, who gave us some excellent soup, vile cutlets, and good macaroni. In the almost pitchy darkness, we felt for our ponies, and were groping our way home, when we passed the hospital in which Dr. Mackay, who came out with us in the *"Shooting Star,"* and who was appointed to the staff from the 12th regiment, resides. We ran up-stairs, and found him, with one or two brother medicos, drinking rum-and-water, and *"smoking a weed."* He made us most welcome; and, from his account of his patients, appears to be working hard and most self-sacrificingly in the good work of trying to alleviate pain. We soon left him to continue our way home. Lord Cardigan, immediately on my arriving at Varna, went to head-quarters to ask Lord Raglan's permission for me to accompany the troops to the Crimea. Lord Cardigan was at the trouble of bringing me Lord Raglan's answer himself. It was a decided negative. *"But,"* added Lord Cardigan (touched perhaps by my sudden burst of tears, for I was so worn and weak!), *"should you think proper to disregard the prohibition, I will not offer any opposition to your doing so."*

Wednesday, 30th. – Too weak to rise. I thank God we remain here to-day, and perhaps to-morrow, as the *"Himalaya"* has not yet come in. Captain George and Major Eman called on me, but I was not able to see them. Two men who marched in with us yesterday are dead of cholera to-day. *"Oh God, in whose hands are the issues of life and death!"*

Thursday, 31st. – I was congratulating myself on the chance of another quiet day, when an aide-de-camp galloped up to say that the *"Himalaya"* had arrived in harbour, and we were to turn out immediately to embark. It was then one o'clock. I tried to rise, but at first could hardly stand, and gave up all hope of packing. As soon as they could be got under weight, the bullock waggons started for the quay. Wrapped in an old hat and shawl, Henry lifted me on my dear, gentle pony's back, and we crept down to Varna. But no embarkation for us that night. Till ten o'clock I waited before our arabas arrived, and our tent was pitched; a kind-hearted woman of the regiment gave me a boa, and at half-past ten we got a little dinner, and turned into bed.

▲ Three officers on the staff of Sir George Brown: Captain Ponsonby, full-length, facing left, standing; Captain Pearson, full-length, facing forward, leaning in doorway; and Captain Markham, full-length, facing right, sitting in chair; all are in front of a building. Photo by Roger Fenton.

CHAPTER III

THE EXPEDITION TO THE CRIMEA

▲ A building next to which is a pile of baskets and a holding pen with horses at the landing place on the cattle pier with ship at dock in Balaklava harbor, also view of the landscape of the hills in the background.

THE EXPEDITION TO THE CRIMEA

"He that has sail'd upon the dark blue sea
Has view'd at times, I ween, a full fair sight,
When the fresh breeze is fair as breeze may be, –
The white sails set – the gallant frigate tight –
Masts, spires, and strand retiring to the right; –
The glorious main expanding o'er the bow, –
The convoy spread, like wild swans in their flight –
The dullest sailor wearing bravely now, –
So gaily curl the waves above each dashing prow!"

Byron

"Ἔπειτα δὲ Κιμμερίοισιν
Νῆα θοὴν ἐπάγοντες ἱκάνομεν."

The Argonauts

*F*riday, September 1st. – The embarkation began at six o'clock. Whilst the troops were filing down, Captain Lockwood, one of Lord Cardigan's *aides-de-camp*, rode up with an order from Lord Lucan that no officer was to embark more than one horse; those who had embarked more were to send them ashore again. Pleasant news this for me! However, I had no time to grumble, but hoisting myself into an araba full of baggage, and disguised as much as possible, I went down to the shore. Lord Lucan, who was there, scanned every woman, to find traces of a lady; but he searched in vain, and I, choking with laughter, hurried past his horse into the boat. Here the crew received me very hospitably, gave me some water, and a compliment on the clearness of my cheeks, which *"did not look as though I had done much hard work in the sun,"* and finally put me safely on board the *"Himalaya,"* where I was immediately handed down to my cabin.

Monday, 4th. – We hoped to sail to-day.

Tuesday, 5th. – I have remained in my cabin ever since I came on board. Well may we pray for *"all prisoners and captives."* After my free life under the *"sweet heavens,"* to be hermetically sealed up in the narrow cabin of a ship – I cannot breathe, even though head and shoulders are thrust out of window.
Since I have been here death has been amongst us. Poor Captain Longmore, who on Friday helped me up the ship's side, was dead on Sunday morning – *"Stretch'd no longer on the rack of this rough world."*
Death with such inexorable gripe appears in his most appalling shape. He was seized but on Friday with diarrhœa, which turned to cholera on Saturday, and on Sunday the body was left in its silent and solemn desolation. During his death struggle the party dined in the saloon, separated from the ghastly wrangle only by a screen. With few exceptions, the dinner was a silent one; but presently the champagne corks flew, and – but I grow sick, I cannot draw so vivid a picture of life and death. God save my dear husband and me from dying in the midst of the din of life!
The very angels must stand aloof. God is our hope and strength, and without Him we should utterly fail. To-day the signal came to proceed to Balchick Bay; and having hooked ourselves on to No. 78., with the Connaught Rangers on board, we steamed to join the flight of ships sailing from Varna. About two hours brought us to Balchick; and the appearance of the bay, crowded with every species of ship, from the three-decker man-of-war down to the smallest river steam-tug, filled the mind with admiration at the magnificent naval resources of England. Delay prevails here as everywhere.
The fleet are all collected and awaiting the order to proceed. Sebastopol is within thirty-six hours' sail, and apparently there is no impediment: but not a vessel has weighed anchor.

▲ Lord Raglan's Head Quarters, with Lord Raglan, Marshal Pélissier, Lord Burghersh, Spahi & Aide-de-camp of Marshal Pélissier

Wednesday, 6th. – Some say we are waiting for the wind to change, or lull; others that we are to wait until the *"Banshee"* arrives with despatches from England. Many more are betting that peace is proclaimed, and that we shall be met at Sebastopol by a flag of truce. I incline to the opinion that we are waiting for the *"Banshee."* The weather continues lovely. The master of the *"Echinga"* came on board to-night, and tells me that Lady Erroll is in his ship, and that she intends remaining on board during the siege. I had fully made up my mind to, and until this unhappy order of *"Only one horse"* threw over all my plans. My husband, too, seems to think that I could not encounter the fatigue on foot, so I fear I must (most reluctantly) consent to follow him by sea to Sebastopol. Our sick list increases frightfully.

Thursday, 7th. – We sailed in company of the fleet, a truly wonderful sight! News arrived last night of the taking of Bomarsund, which put us all in spirits; and as no accident occurred beyond the snapping of a hawser, we made a successful start.

Friday, 8th. – No motion is perceptible in this magnificent ship, though her mighty heart throbs night and day, and there is sufficient sea to make the transport behind us pitch disagreeably. Were it not for the rush of water beneath the saloon windows, I should fancy myself on land. Walking on the deck, between the lines of horses, I cannot fail to have made friends with two or three – one in particular, a fine large Norman-headed chestnut, with a long flowing mane, and such kindly eyes.

Saturday, 9th. – At a signal from the flag-ship, we pulled up to anchor, in order to concentrate the fleet and allow the laggards to come up. Ignorance concerning our movements prevails everywhere, and conjectures are rife. Many absolutely doubt whether Sebastopol is to be our destination or not.
Henry has been very far from well these last few days, and is laid up with an attack of lumbago, particularly unwelcome just now. Dr. Evans, who has been appointed to the regiment, shows very humane feeling; and I trust, under his kind care, my dear husband will soon recover. Poor Connell, our soldier-servant, still lies sick and suffering; but I hear from Sergeant Lynch that he is, if anything, better.

Sunday, 10th. – Still at anchor, 160 miles from Sebastopol. Yesterday, when we stopped our engines, we were nearly meeting with a serious accident. The transport ship behind us, having too short a hawser, and too much way on her, ran into us, smashing our jolly-boat, and crashing through our bulwarks and taffrail like so much brown paper.

Monday, 11th. – The *"Caradoc"* and *"Agamemnon"* have returned. Signals fly from the mast-head of the flag-ship: "Prepare to get under weigh." Discussion of our unknown destination; some say Odessa – some Sebastopol. Sunshine above, and smooth water below. On board not half-a-dozen men feel *"as if they were on the eve of fighting."*

Tuesday, 12th. – At 9, A.M., we came in sight of the Crimea. We have been on board twelve days today. Twelve days accomplishing 300 miles! The delay puzzles as much as it grieves and disgusts. Lord Cardigan, too, is growing very impatient of it. Towards evening the ships drew up closer together. Magnificent two- and three-deckers sailed on each side of the transport fleet. A forest of masts thrust their spear-like heads into the sunset clouds. Birnam Wood is come to Dunsinane! At even-fall, the Brenda, a little Danube boat, drawing four feet of water, was ordered off to Sebastopol to reconnoitre. An answering pendant was run up to her peak: a puff of smoke, a turn of her paddle-wheels, and away flew the little craft, shaking out her white wings like a bird.

Wednesday, 13th. – The entrance to the harbour of Sebastopol is distinctly visible. Every one is roused up and full of energy, except my dear husband, who lies sick and full of pain in his cabin. I much fear he will not be able to land. A signal at twelve o'clock to *"Keep in your station."* We are near enough to the shore to see houses, corn, cattle, and a horse and covered cart. Not a shot has been fired; all is tranquillity in the serene sky above, and the unrippled waters beneath. All are quiet except Lord Cardigan, who is still full of eagerness. Poor Connell is not nearly so well. There is a soldier's wife on board, too, suffering severely from fever. What will become of her when the troops disembark!

Thursday, 14th. – Leaving Eupatoria behind us, we hauled close in shore, about nine o'clock, about thirty miles from Sebastopol. The French began to disembark forthwith, and by ten o'clock the tricolor was planted on the beach. I have a painful record to make. During last night our poor servant Connell, after struggling long with fever, succumbed to it, and closed his eyes, I trust, in peace.

I did not know of his danger till I heard of his death. To-day he was committed to the keeping of the restless sea, until the day when it shall give up its dead.

Friday, 15th. – English troops disembarking in a heavy surf. The landing of the horses is difficult and dangerous. Such men as were disembarked yesterday were lying all exposed to the torrents of rain which fell during the night. How it did rain! In consequence an order has been issued to disembark the tents.

The beach is a vast and crowded camp, covered with men, horses, fires, tents, general officers, staff officers, boats landing men and horses, which latter are flung overboard, and swum ashore. Eleven were drowned today. I am glad to say we lost none. Lord Cardigan begins to be eager for the fray, and will be doing something or other directly he has landed, I fancy. He landed to-day at five.

Saturday, 16th. – All our horses were ashore by half-past ten, and started immediately on outpost-duty, for which they tell me Lord Cardigan has taken a force of Rifles and Artillery as well. At ten o'clock to-day, with failing heart, I parted from my dear husband, and watched him go ashore; whilst I, alas! having no horse, cannot follow him, but must go on board the *"Shooting Star,"* and get round by sea. How I hate it!

How much rather I would endure any hardship than be separated from him at this time! But my reason and strength both tell me it is impracticable, and so I must make up my mind to it. Captain Fraser received me with his usual most considerate kindness, and tried by every means to make me forget my wretched position.

Sunday, 17th. – Artillery disembarking all day from the *"Shooting Star."* One poor fellow caught his hand in a block, and tore it terribly.

Monday, 18th. – To-day I set my foot in the Crimea. A lovely day tempted me to disembark and try to see my dear husband on shore. Captain Fraser and I started at twelve o'clock. On landing amongst the Artillery, we first inquired for the poor fellow who was hurt yesterday, and then for the Light Cavalry. *"They are seven miles inland!!"* I never can forget, or be sufficiently grateful to the officers of Artillery for, the kindness they showed me this day. After looking about for a quiet horse to carry me, they decided on stopping a party of Horse Artillery, and getting them to give us seats on the gun-carriage. Mr. Grylls, who had charge of the party, most courteously assented, and by his kindness I was able to reach the outposts.

Here I surprised my husband, who shares a tent with five officers, and who was delighted to see me. Whilst I remained there, a patrol of the 13th Light Dragoons came in, commanded by Colonel Doherty. They had seen a body of about six hundred Cossacks, who had fired at them, but without effect. These same Cossacks, a few minutes later, had set two of the neighbouring villages, and all the corn, on fire. After about an hour spent in camp, Henry put his regimental saddle on his horse, and I mounted him, Henry and Captain Fraser walking by my side, and we returned to the shore. Our road was lurid with the red glare of the vast fires. This country is as fertile as Bulgaria, and has all the advantages of cultivation. In the village close to the outposts, of which the Rifles had possession, were found comfortable and well-furnished houses, with grand pianofortes, pictures, books, and everything evincing comfort and civilisation. Several of our riflemen have been killed by the Cossacks, who hover round the army like a flying cloud. We reached the beach at dusk; and again taking leave of my husband, with a heavy heart I stepped into the boat and was rowed on board.

Tuesday, 19th. – The troops have all advanced to-day; and about half-past three we heard the heavy sound of the guns booming across the water, as we lay quietly at anchor. What can those guns mean? I wonder if, among the annals of a war, the sickening anxieties of mother, wife, and sister ever find a place. Let us hope the angel of compassion makes record of their tears.

Wednesday, 20th. – Left Kalamita Bay, and, with several other ships, joined the rest of the fleet off Eupatoria.

Thursday, 21st. – Captain Tatham, of the *"Simoom,"* took me ashore in his boat. It was a lovely day.

We walked about Eupatoria; and Captain Tatham introduced me to the governor, Captain Brock, who showed me great kindness and attention. In his house (a very comfortable one, with polished oak floors and large windows) he had safely secured in *"durance vile"* two prisoners, the land steward and shepherd of Prince Woronzow. After leaving Captain Brock, we met a Russian propriétaire – one of the very few who remained in the town. He conversed with us in French for some time, and showed us over the Greek church.

Nearly all the inhabitants, terrified at the apparition of an enemy's fleet, had fled. Captain Brock, in the hope of procuring prompt supplies, has fixed a tariff regulating the price of all kinds of stock; and the Tartar population, delighted at the ready and large circulation of money, bring in provisions freely and willingly. Eupatoria is rather a pretty town, interspersed with trees, with large, low, comfortable-looking, detached houses.

Friday, 22nd. – Was awoke from a restless sleep by the entrance of my maid – a soldier's wife – with her apron over her eyes. I naturally asked what was the matter. *"Oh, ma'am! Captain Tatham has sent to say he has received despatches, which will oblige him to leave Eupatoria to-day. And there has been a dreadful battle – 500 English killed, and 5000 Russians; and all our poor cavalry fellows are all killed; and, the Lord be good to us, we're all widows."* God, and he only, knows how the next hour was passed – until the blessed words, *"O thou of little faith,"* rang in my heart. At breakfast I asked Captain Fraser for the particulars of the message; but he, from a feeling of kindly wishing to save me anxiety, assured me he had heard nothing about the battle, and did not believe a word of it. However, at two o'clock, I went ashore to see the Governor, and ascertain the words of the despatch. He told me that there had been a severe battle at the river Alma, but no official particulars had yet reached him.

Saturday, 23rd. – I heard more particulars of this great fight, though very few: 2090 English killed and wounded; the 7th and 23rd Fusiliers almost destroyed, and, thank God! the Cavalry not engaged.

How can timorous, nervous women live through a time like this! The guns which we heard as we were breasting our swift way from Kalamita to Eupatoria, were merely messengers to us of the heavy firing inland, causing wounds, blood, and sudden death – lives, for which we would gladly give our own, extinguished in a moment; hands flung out in agony, faces calm and still in death; all our prayers unavailing now: no more speech, no more life, no more love.

▲ Interior of sickbay, HMS Belleisle. Cholera was a huge problem in the Crimean war, and naval MOs tried to work out how it behaved and spread. "Water does come up sometimes for consideration as a possible cause, but very often people would attribute it to person-to-person contagion. Or to filthy conditions on a vessel. Or to land winds that may be blowing across a cholera infected area, carrying the seed or the 'germ' to a vessel moored in the Black Sea."

Sunday, 24th. – Again awoke by the guns. Captain Fraser assured me they were the guns of the fleet.

The Cossacks, last night, made a descent upon Eupatoria, and having secured some plunder, fired on our soldiers. Their fire was returned with such interest that they were soon glad to retire. The *"Danube"* steamboat went this afternoon to Katcha, laden with sheep, and taking with her a Russian prisoner – a gentleman – and supposed to be a spy. I met him directly after he was taken, as he was walking from the guard to the shore.

Monday, 25th. – A steamboat came in this morning, and Captain Fraser immediately sent off a boat to the *"Simoom"* (which had not left, as she threatened, on Friday) to ascertain the news. Until as late as six o'clock we had been listening to the guns, but were little prepared for such news as Captain Tatham sent back to us. The fleet are at the Katcha, and the army also. The fleet stood in yesterday, and fired about twenty shots.

The Russians sunk five line-of-battle ships and two frigates across the harbour. Three remain, which cannot get out, nor can we get in. A prisoner reports that all is consternation – Menschikoff in tears.

At Eupatoria news flies from mouth to mouth. They say that, at Alma, the charge of Highlanders was most magnificent; that they swept over the Russian entrenchments like a sea. Our Cavalry being so weak we were unable to follow up our advantage, or we might have cut off the enemy in their retreat. It is said that the whole garrison of Sebastopol was engaged at Alma – 50,000 Russians to about 45,000 English and French. I hear the English bore the brunt of the fight. Went ashore this afternoon, and rode with Captain Brock, who most kindly provides me with both horse and saddle. After we had finished our ride, we went to one of the deserted houses, where we found a grand pianoforte – the first I had played on for so long! It was like meeting a dear and long absent friend. The house and garden were soon filled, and echoing to the magnificent chords of *"Rule Britannia;"* whilst Tennyson's sweet words, *"Break, Break, Break,"* and the *"Northern Star,"* fitted both the occasion and the place. One more song and I must hasten back, to be on board my ship by twilight. Heavy guns are pouring their dull broadsides on our straining ears. What shall the song be, sad and low, or a wild outburst of desperate courage? I have it:–

> *"Non curiamo l'incerto domani:*
> *Se quest'oggi n'è dato goder."*

Tuesday, nine o'clock. – The day rose foggy and gloomy, and my heart, notwithstanding its elation yesterday at the brilliant conduct of our troops, was dull, anxious, and sad. I am engaged to ride with Captain Brock, and am restless to go ashore, in the hope of hearing news. Oh this suspense! How could I be so weak as to allow myself to be separated from my husband? A life-time of anxiety has been crowded into these ten days.

Eight o'clock found me on board the *"Danube,"* steaming, trembling, rushing through the water towards the fleet at Katcha. A note from Captain Tatham, brought up by the *"Danube,"* at three o'clock, induced me to go and see whether I could not get on board the "Star of the South," and so go down to Balaklava with the siege train. I had one hour to decide; and, packing up a few things in a carpet bag, and taking my saddle, I went on board at four o'clock.

September 27th. – Mr. Cator having duly reported my arrival to Admiral Dundas, the admiral did two things: first, he sent on board some excellent white bread, milk, eggs, &c. &c., for breakfast; and, secondly, he proposed either that I should go down to Balaklava in the *"Simoom,"* and so be passed to the *"Star of the South;"* or else, if, as was most probable, this latter ship had been sent to Scutari with wounded, that I should return to Eupatoria, and be sent down by the earliest opportunity.

I decided, therefore, on availing myself of Mr. Cator's kind offer to take me back to Eupatoria, and we started at eleven o'clock. To-day we stood close in shore, on the coast of ALMA. On our right stood heights occupied by the Russian army; on our left the place where our army bivouacked. Huge volumes of thick, smouldering smoke still rolled heavily over the plain.

The *"Albion,"* close in shore, was occupied in removing wounded. Here and there dark masses lay about, war's silent evidence; and over all was the serene heaven, smiling on a lovely landscape, sunny and bright.

And I, too, *"Smil'd to think God's greatness shone around our incompleteness, And round our restlessness – His rest."* The cabin of the *"Danube"* was full of trophies of the fight – helmets pierced with shot and dabbled in blood, little amulets of brass, all blood-stained and soiled, muskets, bayonets, and swords stained with the red rust of blood. We hear that our army have taken Balaklava, after a slight resistance.

Balaklava is a small harbour to the southward of Sebastopol, affording, from its depth and shelter, a wonderful anchorage for ships. This we suppose will be the base of operations; here all our ammunition stores, troops, &c., will be disembarked. They compute the number of men inside Sebastopol at about 16,000.

On arriving at Eupatoria I heard, with feelings of great sorrow, that Colonel Chester and Captain Evans, of the 23rd, are both killed; that Lord Erroll is wounded; and that poor Mrs. Cresswell is a widow.

God help and support her under a blow that would crush me to my grave! The last tidings heard of Mrs. Cresswell were, that she had gone down to Varna in the "War Cloud." I conclude by this time she has gone home, as Captain Cresswell died of cholera on the Monday of the march. Major Wellesley also died about that time, on board the *"Danube;"* and his boxes, sword, hat, &c., were lying in the cabin – a melancholy sight! How full of anxiety I am! About two o'clock we were safely at anchor off Eupatoria. We went ashore. Captain Brock very kindly mounted Mr. Cator and me, and we three rode round the fortifications.

Captain Brock received information, last evening, of 1800 Cossacks within a few miles of the town. We, too, shall have to record the Battle of Eupatoria. The ride over, I adjourned to the *"Shooting Star;"* but during the afternoon I met, and was introduced to, Captain King, of the *"Leander,"* who very kindly asked me to dine to-morrow. Thus ends my birthday! – day ever to be remembered, as on it I saw my first battle-field.

How many more shall I see ere I am a year older? Shall I ever live to see another year? Look on into the winter, with its foreboding of suffering, cold, privation, and gloom! *"What wilt thou become Through yon drear stretch of dismal wandering?"*

September 28th. – The *"Leander's"* boat came for me at two o'clock, and I had a very rough and wet passage on board. I met the captain of the *"Jena,"* a French man-of-war, Colonel D'Osman, in command of the French troops, Captain Brock, &c.; a very agreeable party, at which we were most hospitably entertained.

Friday, 29th. – I take a letter to Henry ashore with me to-day, as I trust to find some means of forwarding it, and I cannot bear the suspense any longer. To-day I am all unnerved; an indefinable dread is on me.

Captain Fraser caught a magnificent Death's-head moth, and gave it to me. I shivered as I accepted it.

This life of absence and suspense becomes at times intolerable. Oh, when shall I rejoin the army, from which I never ought to have been separated! Any hardship, any action, is better than passive anxiety.

A friend of Captain Fraser's, who came on board, tells me that none have had the courage to acquaint Mrs. Cresswell with her loss; and she is actually coming up to Balaklava with troops. Cruel kindness!

Saturday, 30th. – *"Oh that my grief were thoroughly weighed, and my heaviness laid in the balances together, for the sorrows of the Almighty are within me, and terror sets itself in array before me."*

Sunday, 1st October. – The *"Shooting Star"* is under orders for Katcha; and I am engaged to ride with Captain Brock ashore. Not a ripple stirred the water; so, trusting to Captain Fraser's assurance that the ship would not move to-day, I went ashore after breakfast. It was indeed a heavenly day! Our horses sauntered along, and my heart involuntarily looked up, through the radiant sky, to the universal God of peace and war, sunshine and storm! We saw an immense cloud of locusts making for the sea. The air was quite obscured by them.

Returning about one o'clock, what was my dismay to see the *"Shooting Star"* spreading her white wings, and dropping quietly out to sea! Fortunately, the *"Danube"* was going down at two o'clock.

I did not lose a moment, but after taking a most regretful leave of pleasant, cordial Eupatoria, I went once more on board the *"Danube,"* and started in pursuit of the *"Star."* The breeze had got up considerably, and favouring her, we found her at anchor at Katcha when we arrived.

Monday, 2nd *October.* – To-day my adventures have been more amusing still. Not liking a dull day alone on board, I wrote a note to Lord George Paulet, who called on me immediately after breakfast, and took me away to the *"Bellerophon."* Here I was in the middle of a most agreeable, lazy morning, looking out on the sparkling sea, and listening to the wondrous harmonies of a most perfect band, when Admiral Dundas sent on board to say, that if I wished to go down to Balaklava, *"the 'Pride of the Ocean' was then passing with troops, and he would order her to be hove to; but Mrs. Duberly must not keep her waiting a rnoment longer than necessary."* My transit from the Bellerophon (through one of the lower ports), laden with a ham, some miraculous port wine, and all sorts of good things provided by Lord George's kind hospitality, was accomplished in a very short space. The admiral, however, was impatient, and Captain Christie more so. Mr. Cator was sent in the *"Britannia's"* galley to take me on board; and after accomplishing my packing in ten minutes, and taking my desk and carpet bag, I started in the galley and had some difficulty in overtaking the *"Pride of the Ocean."*

Tuesday, 3rd. – We expected a three hours' sail; but the wind dropped, and we were becalmed for four-and-twenty. By three o'clock we were lying almost stationary before the forts of Sebastopol, and within range of the guns. It was a moment not altogether free from nervousness; but no guns molested us, and we passed unharmed. Presently we passed the light off Chersonese. We lay off the point beyond the Monastery of St. George all night; and at morning, the "Simla" came to tow us to our anchorage just outside Balaklava harbour. This anchorage is a wonderful place; the water is extremely deep, and the rocks which bound the coast exceed in ruggedness and boldness of outline any that I ever saw before. The harbour appears completely land-locked. Through a fissure in the cliffs you can just see a number of masts; but how they got in, or will get out, appears a mystery; they have the appearance of having been hoisted over the cliffs, and dropped into a lake on the other side. At three o'clock, tugs came alongside the "Pride of the Ocean," to disembark her troops, the 1st Royals, who, horses and all, were landed before dark.
At dinner, whilst I was quietly eating my soup, I heard some one enter the cabin, and looking up saw Henry, who had heard of my arrival, and had come on board. I need not say that the evening passed happily enough! He brought me a handful of letters, which occupied me till late at night.

▲ 3rd French Zouaves storming and capturing Telegraph Hill at the battle of Alma.

▲ Roger Fenton's photographic van, 1855, Marcus Sparling, Fenton's assistant, is the figure shown seated at the front of the van.

▲ The Ordnance Wharf, Balaklava, 1855, Roger Fenton. Piles of cannon balls on the quayside at Balaklava. Huge supplies of ammunition, or ordnance, were needed for the artillery at the seige of Sebastopol.

CHAPTER IV

BALAKLAVA

▲ Cornet assistant surgeon Henry Wilkin, 11th Hussars. He survived the Charge of the Light Brigade - Photo by Roger Fenton

BALAKLAVA

"Frigida me cohibent Euxini littora ponti;
Dictus ab antiquâ Axenus ille fuit.
Nam neque jactantur moderatis æquora ventis;
Nec placidos portus hospita navis adit.
Sunt circa gentes, quæ prædam sanguine quærunt:
Non minus infidâ terra timetur aquâ.
Nec procul a nobis locus est ubi Taurica dirâ
Cæde pharetratæ pascitur ara Deæ."

OVID.

"Opfer fallen hier,
Weder Lamm noch Stier,
Aber Menschen-Opfer unerhört."

Gœthe.

Wednesday, October 4th. – This morning I landed at Balaklava, having left the *"Pride of the Ocean"* with regret, after endeavouring to express to Captain Kyle my deep sense of the great consideration and kindness he showed me whilst on board his ship. Mr. Cunningham, the admiralty agent, was going on shore, and I availed myself of a seat in his boat, notwithstanding the day was a rough one; and then I learned the entrance to this wonderful harbour, where the ships lay side by side, moored to the shore as thickly as they could be packed. In the afternoon, Henry came down to see me; and scrambling into his regimental saddle – for I had left my own on board the "Shooting Star" – we rode up to see the Cavalry camp. Here I was obliged to confess, though sorely against my will, that it was impossible I could live in the camp. Henry shares his tent with three men. The cold – the impossibility of getting a separate tent, has made me resolve to remain on board ship, and go daily to the camp.

Thursday, 5th. – I rode all over the camp; went on to the Light Division, to the 63rd and 68th; took my first look at Sebastopol from the land as it lay in a hollow about two miles from us. It is a much finer town as seen from the land. The fortifications appear of great strength and number, and the buildings struck me as being large and handsome. They were busy throwing shell into our lines, but the range was too long to do us any harm. The shells fell into a hollow at our feet; and all that I saw exploded harmlessly; though two days before one had burst in a tent of the 68th, killing one man, and wounding two. We returned through the French lines. The French soldiers seemed astonished at the apparition of a lady in their lines, and made various but very flattering remarks thereon. Late at night Mr. Cator arrived in Balaklava, and came on board the *"Star of the South"* to see me.

Friday, 6th. – The *"Shooting Star"* arrived outside Balaklava last evening. Mr. Cator sent off a gig to her for my saddle, which came ashore about twelve, and will save me much fatigue, as I find the big grey and the regimental saddle very tiring, especially in trotting. I hear to-day of poor Dr. Mackay's death with great regret. He died from the effects of over-exertion in the zealous discharge of his arduous duties amongst the sick.

Sunday, 8th. – Lord Cardigan very kindly lent me a horse, and Mr. Cator and I rode up to the front. Here we saw Captain Hillyar, of the Naval Brigade, who is working hard to get his guns into position. These seamen appear to work with the greatest energy and good-will. One meets a gang of them harnessed to a gun, and drawing with all their might and main; or digging at entrenchments, singing, laughing, and working heartily and cheerily. But their experience of camp-life is short indeed in comparison with that of our poor soldiers, with whom they contrast so gaily. Returning home, we met Sir Edmund Lyons, to whom I was introduced, and who asked me to dine with him to-night on board the *"Agamemnon,"* where I met a very old and valued friend, Captain Drummond, of the *"Retribution."* To-day an affair took place which was severely canvassed at dinner. Some Russian Cavalry drove in our out-lying piquet in the morning, and in consequence all the Cavalry, and Captain Maude's troop of H. A., turned out under Lord Lucan.

By judicious generalship, they say, the whole force might have been taken, or severely punished; but a hesitation at the wrong moment allowed them all to retire out of range, after having killed two or three of our men, while they escaped unhurt.

Monday, 9th. – Walked up to camp with Mr. Bosanquet. Found Henry, who accompanied us part of the way back, and then went on board the *"Danube"* to luncheon. Henry and I dined there at six o'clock. In the afternoon I walked along the ridge of the stupendous rocks overlooking the sea. The spray dashed into my face – the sea foamed far beneath my feet. There was something in the strong wind, the beetling cliffs, the churning sea, and boundless view that filled me with glorious admiration and delight.

Last night our dear horses *"Bob"* and *"Whisker"* arrived from Varna, and were taken to the camp this afternoon. I look forward to to-morrow, when I shall see them again.

Tuesday, 10th. – Henry brought down the grey horse, and *"Whisker."* The day was intensely cold, a bitter wind swept through us, chilling every pulse. When we reached the camp, we found poor *"Bob"* half dead with cold; so, shifting the saddles, Henry got on his back, and we stretched away at a rapid canter for the front. Here we met Major Lowe, of the 4th Light Dragoons, and Captain Portal, who asked us to dine.

We gladly accepted; and while dinner was preparing, he rode with us to the extreme right, to show us Sebastopol from a fresh point of view. Close to us, hid in brushwood, was our own piquet; about 1000 yards from us was the Russian piquet. From the forts of Sebastopol the shot and shell came hissing every two minutes. I could not but feel a high degree of excitement, and I think it was not unnatural. We were standing on the brow of a hill, backed by our magnificent troops, and fronting the enemy; the doomed city beneath our feet, and the pale moon above: it was indeed a moment worth a hundred years of every-day existence.

I have often prayed that I might *"wear out my life, and not rust it out,"* and it may be that my dreams and aspirations will be realised.

Wednesday, 11th. – A French transport got aground yesterday before Sebastopol. The Russians fired at her, and carried away her bowsprit. The crew deserted her, but endeavoured to get her off during the night. The garrison made a sortie this morning with the bayonet, but retreated as soon as our men turned out.

Friday, 13th. – A report was current that the fire of the siege was to open to-day, but hardly a shot disturbed the warm serenity of the air. What a variable climate! Three days ago the cold was intense, to-day the sun is oppressive. Captain Lockwood rode down to call on me. He told me with a melancholy face, that the Russians had made a successful descent on Eupatoria, and had wrested the place from us; but a lieutenant in the navy who came in shortly after, declared this information was false, as, although driven back, the force had returned, and effectually driven out the enemy. The arrival of ships from Eupatoria laden with supplies, would seem to say that at any rate the Russians had not possession of it. The *"Cambria"* and *"Medway"* arrived to-day, each with a regiment of 1300 Turks.

Saturday, 14th. – Since last night two yachts have come into harbour, the *"Dryad"* (Lord Cardigan's) and the *"Maraquita"* (Mr. Carew's). What a satire is the appearance of these fairy ships amidst all the rough work of war! They seem as out of place as a London belle would be; and yet there is something very touching in their pretty gracefulness. Henry, Captain Fane, Mr. Goss, R.N., and I started on horseback for the camp.

We lunched at our own tent. Our ride took in nearly the whole front line of the camp, commencing on the right, at the ground lately occupied by the 4th Light Dragoons, passing the Rifles and the 23rd, and then returning by the French. The entrenching work progresses rapidly, under a heavy and continuous fire.

I hear that Lord Raglan was in the foremost trench last night till one o'clock. A rifleman standing near him had his head taken off by a round shot. Either to-day, or yesterday, a rifleman, seeing a shell light in the entrenchment, knocked out the fuse with his rifle. He was mentioned in general orders. I cannot but think it a pity that our service provides no decoration, no distinctive reward of bravery, for such acts as this.

If it were only a bit of red rag, the man should have it, and wear it immediately, as an honourable distinction, instead of waiting for a medal he may never live to obtain, or may only obtain years hence, when it shall have lost half its value. Guns are run into position to-night; the wheels were being muffled in sheep-skin when I was in camp. I heard of a sortie on the French this morning, but no particulars.

Sunday, 15th. – Awoke exhausted. What an exhaustion! It seemed to me as though my life was ebbing away, my sands running quietly down; so I lay for a long time, becalmed in soul and body.

I cannot account for this at all. I remained in this state all the morning, and did not get up till twelve o'clock; at which time Captain Nolan came in, and we had a long and interesting conversation.

After discussing my afternoon's amusement, I determined on accepting his horse and saddle, with a tiger-skin over the holsters; while he borrowed a pony, and we rode together to see Henry at the camp.

After spending an hour in his tent, Henry and I walked down to the *"Star of the South"* to dinner, Henry returning on foot at night.

Monday, 16th. – For three days the firing has been continuous. Captain Nolan told me yesterday that the siege would open in earnest on Tuesday. A party of us sat till late on deck, watching the flashes of the guns.

All night they kept it up, but now, 11 A.M., are quiet. The *"Agamemnon"* steamed out yesterday from Balaklava to join the fleet. The French are at this moment landing a fresh regiment of Cavalry, and the *"Medway"* is being cleared of her cargo of Turks. We wait, with some little excitement, for to-morrow.

I have ordered my horse at eight o'clock in the morning.

Tuesday, October 17th, 10 P.M. – At half past six o'clock began that fearful rain of shot and shell, which poured incessantly on the forts and batteries of Sebastopol, until night befriended the city, and threw her shade over it. At a quarter past seven the Round Tower was silenced, though the battery at its foot still kept up a fire from two guns, which we could not enfilade. Soon after ten Henry and I had arrived, and took our place opposite the Fourth Division. At ten o'clock a French powder magazine exploded, which dismounted fifteen guns, and killed about forty of their men. At half-past one, the French and English fleets, with the *"Mahmoudie,"* brought in their fire. The *"Agamemnon,"* with Sir E. Lyons on board, went close in, followed by the *"Sanspareil."* The *"London,"* *"Albion,"* *"Bellerophon,"* *"Retribution,"* were all more or less severely mauled, as they poured in broadside after broadside, with incredible and incessant noise.

I merely mention the names of such ships as I know something of. There were many others, amongst them the *"Rodney,"* *"Arethusa,"* *"Trafalgar,"* and the *"Tribune."* The *"London"* was twice on fire. The *"Albion"* had a shell which, by unlucky chance, pitched into Captain Lushington's stores, destroying his cellar and his clothes. The *"Bellerophon"* had a shell through Lord George's cabin; the *"Retribution"* lost her mainmast. At ten minutes past three a magnificent sight presented itself – a huge explosion in the Mud Fort (Redan), the smoke of which ascended to the eye of heaven, and then gathering, fell slowly and mournfully down to earth. I thought of torture and sudden death, and was softened to tears, while round me cheers burst from every throat – *"All down the line one deafening shout."* Officers and men were carried away with enthusiasm, and I felt myself half cheering too. Three quarters of an hour after a smaller explosion caught our eye.

Again the cheer rang out. *"Men! Men, for God's sake! It is ours!"* and an ammunition-waggon sent up its contents to form a fierce cloud in the serene sky. We left at dusk, and rode slowly down to Balaklava, our hearts and ears filled with the magnificent din of war. Our casualties have been very few.

Poor Captain Rowley and the assistant-surgeon of the 68th are dead. The gathering twilight prevented our seeing much of the damage done to the town. We fancied it greater than it proved. One of our Lancaster guns burst to-day; the other is doing good work. The shot rushes with such vehement noise through the air that it has been surnamed the *"Express Train."* We fired 170 rounds a gun yesterday (so they say). I was not sorry to find rest on board ship, being tired out with the excitement and exertion of the day.

▲ View of landing place and people working at ordnance wharf, Balaklava harbor, with ships, buildings, and Genoese Castle in background.

Wednesday, 18th. – Did not intend going out early, but at nine o'clock I saw my horse saddled on the beach. A large Russian force is collected on the plains, at whom, as is evident, we are firing hard.

I dressed in all haste, and started to the front. Here I found Cavalry, Artillery, and Turks drawn up beyond our camp, and a Russian force in the valley, at some 1,800 yards distance, standing gazing at them. The firing had all ceased, and the greater part of the Russians had retired under shelter of a hill. As soon as we were tired of looking at them, and tired of waiting for them to advance, we left the field battery, behind which we had taken our places, and went slowly on to the front. The French batteries were unable to reopen fire.

The ships were a great deal too much mauled yesterday to be able to go in again for some time.

The English guns were firing, and we had some red-hot shot, in the hopes of setting fire to the town; but the town appears built of incombustible materials, although it was twice slightly on fire yesterday, the flames were almost immediately extinguished I am told that the men of Captain Lushington's battery last night refused to be relieved, though they had been at work all day. They said they had *"got their range, and were doing good work, and would not go away, – all they wanted was something to eat, and some grog."* Sir George Cathcart sent them down immediately all the food and grog he could muster. *"Ah!"* exclaimed one of the riflemen who had been firing at the gunners in the Mud Fort before the explosion took place, *"When it blew up, in the confusion, there was beautiful shooting!"* We had luncheon in Major Wynne's tent, of the 68th, and left again about three o'clock to ride back to Balaklava. Passing the fortifications between the front and rear, we found the French mustered in rather a strong force in the battery overlooking the Russian army.

No movement had been made by the Russians. They will probably remain in the shelter of the hill until they are drawn. Artillery and Cavalry were coming slowly home as we approached our lines. The heavy guns of the siege still follow us with their ceaseless sound. Colonel Hood, of the Guards, was killed to-day, and the ambulance corps brought down forty sick, to be embarked on board ship at Balaklava. I saw, with the aid of glasses, to-day a loose horse going with a strange halting gait before the batteries of the Russian forts. He was thought to be an English Artillery horse wounded yesterday; strange that, among all that thunder of shot and shell, not one bullet could be spared for him.

Thursday, 19th. – We thought Sebastopol to stand, perhaps, a three days' siege – more likely a single day's; while some, more arrogant still, allowed it eight hours to resist the fury of the allies! Now there are orders that no shot is to be fired into the town for fear of destroying the houses. Is this because Lord Raglan is confident of the speedy possession of the town, or from the estimable amiability of his private character, which makes him shrink from inflicting wanton damage or death? This order to spare the town is much commented on. However commendable the greatest humanity may be, we cannot but remember that the blood of 2090 men, lying on the field of Alma, calls to us from the ground. Were we besieged, the Russians would not show the like consideration to us. To-day we moved our camp, so as to be out of the way of the batteries we have erected on the heights round Balaklava. I did not go to the front to-day. I got sick with anxiety, and deaf with the guns.

Friday, 20th. – To-day the French siege-guns are in good play, and firing with good aim. They commenced their rocket-practice about two o'clock, and created a fire in the direction of the harbour. The battery at the foot of the Round Tower is still working away, though the Round Tower itself has been silenced since seven o'clock in the morning of the siege. The French silenced a square fort on the left early to-day. As we rode home, we found the Russian army had moved out again, and all our forces were outposted in the batteries and at the top of the hills. However, I was too hungry to stay and watch them, and left them to look at each other at their leisure. There is a talk of storming the town to-morrow. I fancy, if it was intended, it would not be talked about beforehand. A deserter reports that the troops inside are in fear and disheartened; if so, an assault may not be necessary. Major Norcott, of the Rifles, to whom I was talking to-day, gave me a most affecting account of the death of his favourite horse at Alma. He spoke with his eyes filled with tears; and, indeed, he could hardly have found a more sympathising auditor, for I never think of my own dear grey without a sharp and cruel pain. A sailor in one of the naval batteries was wounded yesterday. But *"he wasn't going to be carried about as long as he could walk;"* and he actually crawled to the 68th camp, and asked for a *"drink of water."* Individual instances of courage are too many for me to record separately.

Saturday, 21st. – Hearing that nothing more than the usual fire was going on at the front, I did not hurry forward to-day, but reached my usual ground of observation in time to see an explosion behind the Round Tower, followed by a heavy fire from the two unsilenceable guns, which they kept up viciously for some time. The Russian fire was slack, and principally directed on the French lines. The French batteries are firing well. Sir George Cathcart, with whom I was in conversation for some time, tells me that no attempt must be made to storm the town now, until the French are ready to act in concert with us. All appear to concur in thinking that the Crimea will be our winter quarters. A very promising officer, Mr. Greathed, was killed in the naval battery to-day.

Sunday, 22nd. – Guns as usual.

Monday, 23rd. – Rode up to the battery on the left; I do not know which it was. Last night the men were making a new parallel, 500 yards in advance of the present ones. At what an enormous range (it appears to me) we have placed our guns! Will this long range answer? I think the siege progresses very slowly. They ran the Lancaster in and pointed it on the dockyards. A sortie was made this morning on the French. Their first intimation of it was from a party of soldiers appearing on the embrasures, crying out, *"Ne tirez pas! nous sommes Anglais!"* Before the French discovered their mistake they had spiked three guns. A sortie was also made on our piquets, led on most gallantly by a Russian officer. He was shot in the mouth, and taken prisoner. Captain Brown, of the 44th, lost his right arm and two fingers of his left hand.

Tuesday, 24th. – Awful confusion, hurry, and noise in the harbour of Balaklava, facilitating (?) the disembarkation of twenty-four pound shot and powder. Some Artillery officers, who lunched on board the *"Star of the South,"* speak much of the fatigue consequent on the work in the trenches.

Our batteries succeeded in setting fire to a part of the town at half-past three, P.M., which burnt fiercely for a short time, but was eventually extinguished. A flag of truce was sent to our head-quarters to-day, to say that the sick and wounded were distributed in various houses in Sebastopol, which should be distinguished by a yellow flag, and to request that they might be exempt from fire; but Lord Raglan, fancying this merely a scheme to make magazines of such houses, refused to comply with the proposal.

Wednesday, 25th. – Feeling very far from well, I decided on remaining quietly on board ship to-day; but on looking through my stern cabin windows, at eight o'clock, I saw my horse saddled and waiting on the beach, in charge of our soldier-servant on the pony. A note was put into my hands from Henry, a moment after.

It ran thus: *"The battle of Balaklava has begun, and promises to be a hot one. I send you the horse. Lose no time, but come up as quickly as you can: do not wait for breakfast."*

Words full of meaning! I dressed in all haste, went ashore without delay, and, mounting my horse *"Bob,"* started as fast as the narrow and crowded streets would permit. I was hardly clear of the town, before I met a commissariat officer, who told me that the Turks had abandoned all their batteries, and were running towards the town. He begged me to keep as much to the left as possible, and, of all things, to lose no time in getting amongst our own men, as the Russian force was pouring on us; adding, *"For God's sake, ride fast, or you may not reach the camp alive."* Captain Howard, whom I met a moment after, assured me that I might proceed; but added, *"Lose no time."*

Turning off into a short cut of grass, and stretching into his stride, the old horse laid himself out to his work, and soon reaching the main road, we clattered on towards the camp. The road was almost blocked up with flying Turks, some running hard, vociferating, *"Ship Johnny! Ship Johnny!"* while others came along laden with pots, kettles, arms, and plunder of every description, chiefly old bottles, for which the Turks appear to have a great appreciation. The Russians were by this time in possession of three batteries, from which the Turks had fled. The 93rd and 42nd were drawn up on an eminence before the village of Balaklava. Our Cavalry were all retiring when I arrived, to take up a position in rear of their own lines.

Looking on the crest of the nearest hill, I saw it covered with running Turks, pursued by mounted Cossacks, who were all making straight for where I stood, superintending the striking of our tent and the packing of our valuables. Henry flung me on the old horse; and seizing a pair of laden saddle-bags, a great coat, and a few other loose packages, I made the best of my way over a ditch into a vineyard, and awaited the event.

For a moment I lost sight of our pony, *"Whisker,"* who was being loaded; but Henry joined me just in time to ride a little to the left, to get clear of the shots, which now began to fly towards us. Presently came the Russian Cavalry charging, over the hill-side and across the valley, right against the little line of Highlanders. Ah, what a moment! Charging and surging onward, what could that little wall of men do against such numbers and such speed? There they stood. Sir Colin did not even form them into square. They waited until the horsemen were within range, and then poured a volley which for a moment hid everything in smoke.

The Scots Greys and Inniskillens then left the ranks of our Cavalry, and charged with all their weight and force upon them, cutting and hewing right and left.

A few minutes – moments as it seemed to me – and all that occupied that lately crowded spot were men and horses, lying strewn upon the ground. One poor horse galloped up to where we stood; a round shot had taken him in the haunch, and a gaping wound it made. Another, struck by a shell in the nostrils, staggered feebly up to *"Bob,"* suffocating from inability to breathe. He soon fell down. About this time reinforcements of Infantry, French Cavalry, and Infantry and Artillery, came down from the front, and proceeded to form in the valley on the other side of the hill over which the Russian Cavalry had come.

Now came the disaster of the day – our glorious and fatal charge. But so sick at heart am I that I can barely write of it even now. It has become a matter of world history, deeply as at the time it was involved in mystery. I only know that I saw Captain Nolan galloping; that presently the Light Brigade, leaving their position, advanced by themselves, although in the face of the whole Russian force, and under a fire that seemed pouring from all sides, as though every bush was a musket, every stone in the hill side a gun. Faster and faster they rode. How we watched them! They are out of sight; but presently come a few horsemen, straggling, galloping back. *"What can those skirmishers be doing? See, they form up together again. Good God! it is the Light Brigade!"*

At five o'clock that evening Henry and I turned, and rode up to where these men had formed up in the rear. I rode up trembling, for now the excitement was over. My nerves began to shake, and I had been, although almost unconsciously, very ill myself all day. Past the scene of the morning we rode slowly; round us were dead and dying horses, numberless; and near me lay a Russian soldier, very still, upon his face.

In a vineyard a little to my right a Turkish soldier was also stretched out dead. The horses, mostly dead, were all unsaddled, and the attitudes of some betokened extreme pain. One poor cream-colour, with a bullet through his flank, lay dying, so patiently!

Colonel Shewell came up to me, looking flushed, and conscious of having fought like a brave and gallant soldier, and of having earned his laurels well. Many had a sad tale to tell. All had been struck with the exception of Colonel Shewell, either themselves or their horses. Poor Lord Fitzgibbon was dead.

Of Captain Lockwood no tidings had been heard; none had seen him fall, and none had seen him since the action. Mr. Clutterbuck was wounded in the foot; Mr. Seager in the hand. Captain Tomkinson's horse had been shot under him; Major De Salis's horse wounded. Mr. Mussenden showed me a grape-shot which had *"killed my poor mare."* Mr. Clowes was a prisoner. Poor Captain Goad, of the 13th, is dead.

Ah, what a catalogue! And then the wounded soldiers crawling to the hills! One French soldier, of the Chasseurs d'Afrique, wounded slightly in the temple, but whose face was crimson with blood, which had dripped from his head to his shoulder, and splashed over his white horse's quarters, was regardless of the pain, but rode to find a medical officer for two of his *"camarades,"* one shot through the arm, the other through the thigh. Evening was closing in. I was faint and weary, so we turned our horses, and rode slowly to Balaklava. We passed Mr. Prendergast, of the Scots' Greys, riding down to the harbour, wounded in the foot; the pluck with which an Englishman puts pain out of the question is as wonderful as it is admirable.

Time would fail me to enumerate even the names of those whose gallantry reached my ears. Captain Morris, Captain Maude, both cut and shot to pieces, and who have earned for themselves an imperishable name!

What a lurid night I passed. Overcome with bodily pain and fatigue, I slept, but even my closed eyelids were filled with the ruddy glare of blood.

▲ The charge of the light cavalry brigade at Balaklava, the 25th October 1854. Artwork by William Simpson.

Thursday, 26th. – They are sending as many ships as possible out of harbour. On board the ship in which I live are 400 tons of gunpowder, and she is to be gradually filled up. The Russians, to the number of 5000, made a sortie on the French lines this morning, but were repulsed with loss. Two Russian officers, wounded yesterday, were brought: down and embarked to-day from Balaklava. No tidings of Captain Lockwood.

They tell me that there is a chance that Captain Morris may survive, and that poor Maude, though seriously, is not mortally wounded. I wrote to his wife to-day, to endeavour to break to her, as best I could, the fact that he was only wounded! My poor servant, whose husband was in the 8th, has been in deep anxiety and distress, as, when I left last night, her husband had not been seen. One man told me he thought he saw him fall; but, of course, I would give her no information but facts. To-day, hearing that he had returned wounded, and was in hospital, she started to see if it was true. Alas, poor woman! all she heard was tidings of his death.

Mr. Cator walked over from Khersonnese to-night, and arrived about nine o'clock.

Saturday, 28th. – What an anxious night. Guns firing incessantly from the batteries round Balaklava! and occasional volleys of musketry seemed to say that the enemy were having another try for it. I lay awake, a little anxious and doubtful. The harbour was astir – steamers getting up their steam, anchors being weighed, and all made ready for departure. If they should be able to shell the harbour! The *"Star of the South"* is full of powder, and every ship has more or less on board. Daylight brought news that upwards of 200 horses had escaped from the Russian lines, and galloped towards our entrenchments and those of the French.

The marines, thinking, in the dark, that it was a charge of Cavalry, fired right and left; the affrighted horses, turning off, dashed over the plain towards the French, who opened on them immediately. Many were killed, but many more, rushing over everything, were caught in the camp, and distributed – a welcome windfall after the 25th. A flag of truce went into Sebastopol to-day, to enquire the number of officers taken, and their fate and names. The answer was, that eleven officers were captured, of whom only two survive.

Who may those two be? We are to send again to-morrow to learn their names. Lord Cardigan tells me, that the loss of the Light Brigade in the charge was 300 men, 24 officers, and 354 horses. Twenty-seven wounded horses have since been shot. Lord Cardigan received a slight lance wound in the side; he distinguished himself by the rapidity with which he rode. Shifted camp to-day to be out of the way of the French guns.

Sunday, 29th. – Tremendous gale of wind all last night. Fortunately it blew off shore, or it might have caused serious damage among the ships lying outside. Why are the ships allowed to lie outside? All the transport masters object to the anchorage. Why are they kept there against their judgments and their will? Saw Colonel Lake and Mr. Grylls yesterday, for the first time since they so kindly assisted me in my search for Henry, at Kalamita. The flag of truce went in again to-day, and returned answer that Mr. Clowes, 8th Hussars, and Mr. Chadwick, 17th Lancers, were the only survivors. Poor Lockwood!

Wednesday, November 1st. – A bright, cheery day in harbour tempted me to ride to the camp. Oh, false valley of Balaklava, to conceal amongst thy many surrounding hills the bitter cold of the higher lands!

Auctions of deceased officers' effects occupied almost every one to-day. The prices were fabulous. An old forage cap fetched 5l. 5s. 0d.; an old pair of warm gloves, 1l. 7s. 0d.; a couple of cotton nightcaps, 1l. 1s. 0d.: whilst horses sold as absurdly cheap – one fetched 12l. 0s. 0d. and another, 9l. A common clasp knife fetched 1l. 10s. 0d. Reinforcements of French troops, Guards, and Highlanders, to the amount of 2000, arrived to-day. Osten Sacken, with a force of 20,000 men, has come to the relief of the besieged city. We are doing nothing particular to-day beyond firing red-hot shot. All are in expectation of the storming, and all, meanwhile, shivering with cold. Henry succeeded in purchasing a very large waterproof wrapper for "Bob," which makes me much easier on his account; but, Oh! how anxious do I feel as often as I look at that dear old friend, and think of the hardships he has to undergo.

Sunday, 5th. – I heard very heavy and continuous firing, which lasted all the morning; but as I saw no one from the front, and Henry was there with his regiment, I could learn nothing about it before twelve o'clock. Then, indeed, news came in fast. At five o'clock this morning, in the middle of a dense fog, our out-lying piquets suddenly found themselves surrounded and fired at from all sides – heavy guns, of large calibre, with shell and musketry, ploughing in every direction. How can I describe the horrors and glories of that day? It was a hand-to-hand battle, wherein every man fought for his life. Stunned, and confused for a moment, our troops rallied with inconceivable energy and courage. From five, A.M., till three in the afternoon they fought with all the acharnement of wild beasts – *"Groom fought like noble, squire like knight, As dauntlessly and well."* But I! – I only knew that Henry was there; and begging Captain Buckley, of the Fusilier Guards, who was recovering from his wound at Alma, and on board the *"Star of the South,"* to accompany me, we started on foot for the front. With such work going on, reports were not likely to be slack. I had barely left the town before I was told of the utter destruction of the Cavalry, which had *"remained the whole day passive under a galling fire."* But I had learnt experience, and this did not trouble me much. We pushed on, and met a cart coming down slowly: in it was Sir George Brown, wounded in the arm. A melancholy train of ambulance was winding slowly down to Balaklava. Alas! I well knew its ghastly freight. An hour later, and Henry was giving me himself an account of the terrible casualties of the day. He spoke with grief of Sir George Cathcart, who bravely met with a soldier's highest honour – a death won with such impetuous courage that the memory of it must last throughout all time. The brigade of Guards has suffered cruelly. General Strangways is dead; poor Major Wynne, of the 68th; Major Dalton, of the 49th, who leaves a young widow and children alone at Constantinople. But who is not among the list of dead? Poor young Cleveland, with his fair, boyish face! Ah me! how ruthless is the sword! I cannot hope to glean full and correct particulars of this day, wondrous in the world's history, until time has allowed the feeling of excitement a little to subside.

Monday, 6th. – Henry and I rode up to our camp, which is situated near the windmill at the front. Here we met le Baron de Noe, who, with Henry, rode on to inspect the battle-field. I could not go. The thought of it made me shudder and turn sick. On his return, Henry told me that the field of Alma was child's play to this! Compressed into a space not much exceeding a square half-mile, lay about 5000 Russians, some say 6000; above 2000 of our own men, exclusive of French, of whom, I believe, there were near 3000; lines upon lines of Artillery horses, heaps upon heaps of slain, lying in every attitude, and congregated in masses – some on their sides, others with hands stiffening on the triggers of their muskets; some rolled up as if they died in mortal pain, others smiling placidly, as though still dreaming of home: while round the batteries, man and horse piled in heaps, wounds and blood – a ghastly and horrible sight! We were taken by surprise, attacked where we had no intrenchment or fortification of any kind. We fought as all know Englishmen will fight; and our loss was in proportion to the carelessness that permitted the attack, rather than to the magnificent courage that repelled it.

Wednesday, November 8th. – The 46th, under Colonel Garrett, arrived in Balaklava to-day, and disembarked this afternoon. They are a particularly fine looking regiment; two companies are already here. They landed 750 strong.

Thursday, 9th. – Rode up to the front to-day with Captain Sayer and Mr. Rochfort, who took up their quarters yesterday on board the *"Star of the South;"* the former having come out to see his brother, who was wounded at *"Alma,"* and the latter as an amateur. They went to inspect the horrors of the battle-field; Henry and I went to Sir George Cathcart's grave – fit resting-place for the heart of such a soldier. In the centre of what has been a ruined fortification, in front of the division he led so gallantly, almost within range of the guns of Sebastopol, surrounded by those officers of his division who fell by his side, he sleeps until the reveillée of the Great Day. A cross, rudely built of rough stones, stands at the head of his grave.

Friday, 10th. – A heavy gale of wind made terrible disturbance among the shipping, both inside and outside the harbour, so much so that several ships' masters outside protested at not being admitted to the shelter of the harbour. Owing to the heavy rain, the roads were nearly impassable on Wednesday and to-day. I hear that several of the poor, starved, worn-out Artillery horses died on the road, vainly endeavouring to drag up guns to the front.

Saturday, 11th. – The 62nd regiment landed to-day at Kamiesh Bay. The severe weather affects both men and horses terribly; of the latter, I fear, few will survive to feel the warm breath of spring. These horses have no clothing, and very insufficient food; and the men live in a state that few of our paupers in England would endure.

Monday, 13th. – The "Jura" arrived to-day. It is still blowing as if it never blew before, and raining in torrents. The Russians made a sortie last night on the French, and were repulsed – with what loss, on either side, I am unable to learn.

Tuesday, 14th. – The most terrific gale commenced blowing at about five o'clock this morning.

At seven o'clock, when I looked through the stern-cabin windows, the harbour was seething and covered with foam, and the ships swinging terribly. By nine it had increased to a frightful extent, and I could hardly, even when clinging to the ship, keep my footing on deck. The spray, dashing over the cliffs many hundred feet, fell like heavy rain into the harbour. Ships were crushing and crowding together, all adrift, all breaking and grinding each other to pieces. The stern-work of the *"Star of the South"* was being ground away by the huge sides of the *"Medway,"* which was perpetually heaving against her. By ten o'clock we heard that the most fearful wrack was going on outside amongst the ships at anchor, and some of the party – Captain Sayer, Mr. Rochfort, and Captain Frain – started for the rocks to try if by any means they could save life.

The next tidings were, that the *"Prince"* and the *"Resolute,"* the *"Rip van Winkle,"* the *"Wanderer,"* the *"Progress,"* and a foreign barque, had all gone down, and, out of the whole, not a dozen people saved. At two o'clock, in spite of wind and weather, I managed to scramble from ship to ship, and went ashore to see this most disastrous sight. Ah me! such a sight, once seen, who can forget!

At the moment after my arrival, the devoted and beautiful little clipper ship *"Wild Wave"* was riding to her death. Her captain and crew – all but three small boys – had deserted her at nine o'clock; and she was now, with all her masts standing, and her helpless freight on board, drifting with her graceful outlines and her heart of oak, straightway to her doom. She is under our feet. God have mercy on those children now!

Captain Frain, Captain Liddell, and some seamen heave a rope downwards, at which one boy springs, but the huge wave is rolling backwards, and he is never seen again. A second time they hurl it down to the boy standing on the stern frame, but the ship surging down upon the ruthless rocks, the deck parts beneath his feet, and he is torn, mangled, and helpless; but clinging still, until a wave springs towards him eagerly, and claims him for the sea. The third and last survivor catches at the friendly rope, and swooning with exhaustion and fear, he is laid upon the rock; while in a moment, with one single bound, the little ship springs upwards, as though she, too, was imploring aid, and falls back a scattered mass, covering the sea with splinters, masts, cargo, hay, bread, and ropes. Meantime the *"Retribution,"* the *"Lady Valiant,"* the *"Melbourne,"* the *"Pride of the Ocean,"* the *"Medora,"* the *"Mercia,"* and several more, are all more or less damaged, and. most of them entirely dismasted, riding it out as best they may. The greatest praise is due to the crew of the *"Avon's"* life-boat, who went out fearlessly to endeavour to render aid; but were unable, owing to the heavy sea, to get near the ships. Let me shut up my book; for the more I contemplate it, the more terrible the disaster appears. Captain Jennings, who came on board ill to-day, talks of beds and clothing carried bodily into the air, and of tents being split to ribbons, or torn from the ground, and hurled away. This is nine o'clock, P.M.

The *"Medway,"* *"Marmion,"* *"Brenda,"* and *"Harbinger"* are still hard at work on the sides of our unlucky ship; and I much fear the figure-head of the *"Medway"* will be into my cabin to-night.

Wednesday, 15th. – The sky is serene and blue, and nature, weary of her hurricane of tears, has sobbed herself into quietness. Captain Kyle, of the *"Pride of the Ocean,"* came into harbour this morning, having, together with his crew, abandoned his ship. How beautifully she rode through yesterday's gale! all her masts cut away, and her long black hull, with its graceful lines, sitting on the troubled water like a bird. The *"Retribution"* rode out the gale safely, though holding by only one cable.

Thursday, November 16th. – Report mentions twelve ships lost at Katcha, and thirteen at Eupatoria, but as yet this wants confirmation. To-day one of the crew of the *"Star of the South,"* Welsh by name, has been indefatigable in endeavouring to save the lives of some poor fellows who had been cast on the lower rocks, where they were scarcely to be got at from the heights above. About twelve o'clock, we heard that this fine fellow, in endeavouring to reach a sailor below him, lost his balance, and was lying with a broken leg close to the man he had risked his life to save. A party went to fetch him in, and found him suffering only from contusion, and not from a broken limb. The man appears to have behaved with wonderful courage and good feeling, and is deserving of unqualified praise.

▲ Captain Phillips & Lieutenant Yates, 8th Hussars.

Saturday, November 18th. – A day like the renewal of youth! – cloudless, warm, and so bright! Captain Howard, of the 44th, took pity on me, a prisoner on board ship, and sent down a white Spanish horse for me to ride. I went to the camp, and found them all spreading themselves out to dry in the sunshine, like so many torpid flies. Henry applied to be allowed an office in Balaklava, so as to secure a stable for *"Bob,"* who is half starved and as rough as a terrier. The grey horse was stolen two days ago, and is not yet recovered.

Sunday, 19th. – A mail has arrived. I thirst for letters from England, as a feverish man thirsts for a draught of water. On Friday the Cavalry horses had one handful of barley as their day's food. Yesterday they had the same.

Monday, 20th. – Heavy rain. The 97th landed to-day. They look fresh and well; but I should fancy few will be so to-morrow morning, if this is to be their inauguration day in camp.

Wednesday, 22nd. – Yesterday the *"Queen of the South"* disembarked draughts of Guards, &c., to the amount of 800 men. They were hardly disembarked before nightfall, and as we were returning at dusk from a ride to the camp, we met them marching up. Henry and I had an adventure to-day, exciting though harmless.

We were riding slowly across the plain, under the French batteries, but in full view of the Russian force, when I saw a fragment of shell lying on the ground, and forgetting all about the Russian Artillery, requested Henry to pick it up; he dismounted for the purpose, when luckily I turned round in time to see the smoke of a piece of field artillery. I need hardly say we lost no time in taking ourselves out of range! We were both on white horses, and afforded a conspicuous mark. Lord George Paget is gone home. Thirty-eight other officers, profiting by his example, have sent in their papers.

Thursday, 23rd. – Perpetual sounds of heavy firing during the night told us that something was on hand; and next morning we heard that the Rifles had attacked a battery of twenty guns, but owing to insufficient numbers, they were three times driven back, until a French reinforcement enabled them to hold it.

A very intelligent French soldier of the 20ième de la Ligne came into our tent to-day, when we were up in camp. He had read part of *"Byron,"* and the *"Vicar of Wakefield!"* He told us that on the 5th several of our men, in the confusion, lost their regiments, and placing themselves in the French ranks, fought side by side with their neighbours and allies. Poor Colonel Shewell, overcome at last by the rough life, has been obliged to make up his mind to remain for some days on board ship. The appearance of the officers very much resembles that of the horses; they all look equally thin, worn, ragged, and out of condition in every way.

Sunday, 26th. – A brilliant morning induced us to try and attend church on board the *"Sanspareil."* Arrived there, we were told there was no service, all the men being employed ashore. We stayed for some time in the ward room, looking at the many scars left in the good ship's timbers by the shells on the 17th of October, when she followed the Agamemnon so closely into action. In the afternoon Captain Anderson, Mr. Goss, and I went to service in the chaplain's room in Balaklava, – an interesting congregation enough, composed entirely of soldiers who had come fresh from the noise of war. The quiet voice of the chaplain was inexpressibly soothing, and the words he chose peculiarly applicable to the excited and half-tired state of my mind – *"There remaineth therefore a rest."* He spoke for ten minutes, though at times his voice was barely audible amidst all the din and noise on the quay, the flogging of jaded and dying horses, and the voices of the soldiers, cursing with every imaginable oath their exhausted cattle. The grey horse, *"Job,"* died this evening of sheer starvation: his tail had been gnawed to a stump by his hungry neighbours at piquet.

Misfortune appears to haunt us, as this is the third horse we have lost since leaving England: but we will *"live misfortune down,"* with that dreary and desperate courage that the terrible scenes of this terrible life impart. Poor *"Job!"* he earned his name from his exhaustless patience under innumerable afflictions: he was an enormous, powerful, and hungry horse, and he sold his life by inches. There was no help for it: had it been myself instead of him, I must have died.

Tuesday, 28th. – Captain Dawson Damer came down this afternoon; and I rode back with him to Kadekoi, where the officers of the Guards have a house, and dined there, Henry joining us from the camp. The excellent dinner and kindly hospitality put us quite in spirits, after the ship food and our long fit of depression. Major Hamilton lent me his white pony. Oh, dainty pony! with black lustrous eyes, and little prancing feet, and long white tail dyed red with henna, like the finger tips of the most delicate lady in Stamboul! We rode home at dark, along the rotten, deep, almost impracticable track. The dead horses lying right across the road, as they fell, and the dead and dying bullocks, filled me with horror, and the white pony with spasms of fear. Now we trod upon the muddy carcass of a horse; now we passed a fallen mule, and a huge bullock, sitting up, with long ghastly horns pointing upwards in the moonlight, awaiting his death. No horse is permitted to be destroyed without a special order from Lord Lucan, except in case of glanders, and, I believe, a broken leg. Some horses in our lines have been lying steeped in mud, and in their death-agony, for three days!

Thursday, November 30th. – Tempted by the sunshine, I left my work, and walked over the cliffs with Captain Damer. My work (what will the young ladies at home say to my fingers?) is an enormous canvass sheet and breastplate, which I have made to cover up *"Bob,"* and which I must take to-morrow to the *"Sanspareil"* to

▲ The English and French fleets of the Black Sea

have waterproofed. I was scarcely over the ship's side, when the boat drifted – oh, horror! – against a dead body, one of the many that were floating in from the wrecks outside. It was the first I had happened to see. The Times of the 13th is in harbour, and somebody, I forget who, tells me that my name appears in it. I wish they could put in that I had left the ship, and was established on shore, if only in a single room. Of this, however, I fear there is but little chance, as I hear Balaklava is to be given up to the sick.

The place stinks already with the number of sick Turks, who have turned it into a half-putrid hospital.

I never saw people die with such a dreary perseverance as these Turks. Two hundred of them were buried in one day a short time since. I am happy to hear that it is at last arranged to bring the Light Cavalry down from the front, and quarter them near Balaklava, it being found impossible to convey forage up to them at the front. Fifteen of our horses died last night.

Sunday, December 3rd. – It rained viciously all day. Captain Buckley came down to see me in the afternoon. I hear the sick are dying at an average of eighty per diem. I know that the mortality amongst the newly-arrived regiments is very great; nor can any one wonder at it! We, who are acclimatised, can hardly make head against the hardships of the life, – what, then, must those feel who have just left an English barrack, or even the crowded discomforts of a transport! With some little horror (not much), and a great deal of curiosity, I watched from over the taffrail of the "Star of the South," the embarkation of some Russian prisoners and English soldiers (all wounded) for Scutari. The dignified indifference of the medical officer, who stood with his hands in his pockets, gossiping in the hospital doorway, – the rough and indecent way in which the poor howling wretches were hauled along the quay, and bundled, some with one, and others with both legs amputated, into the bottom of a boat, without a symptom of a stretcher or a bed, was truly an edifying exemplification of the golden rule, *"Do to others as you would be done by."* On board the steam-ship *"Avon,"* I hear the sights and sounds are too dreadful to imagine. An officer, who was sick on board, tells me the wounded men were laid on the deck with nothing but a blanket between them and the boards. Oh, how their wounded limbs must have ached! He said the groans and moans of these poor creatures, on the first night he spent on board, were heart-rending; but by the next night the noise had considerably decreased – death had been more merciful to their pain than man. Independently of the wounded soldiers, with whom our hospitals are full – the dreary, weary Turks have got a kind of plague amongst them, which infects the air. If any body should ever wish to erect a *"Model Balaklava"* in England, I will tell him the ingredients necessary. Take a village of ruined houses and hovels in the extremest state of all imaginable dirt; allow the rain to pour into and outside them, until the whole place is a swamp of filth ancle-deep; catch about, on an average, 1000 sick Turks with the plague, and cram them into the houses indiscriminately; kill about 100 a-day, and bury them so as to be scarcely covered with earth, leaving them to rot at leisure – taking care to keep up the supply. On to one part of the beach drive all the exhausted bât ponies, dying bullocks, and worn-out camels, and leave them to die of starvation. They will generally do so in about three days, when they will soon begin to rot, and smell accordingly. Collect together from the water of the harbour all the offal of the animals slaughtered for the use of the occupants of above 100 ships, to say nothing of the inhabitants of the town, – which, together with an occasional floating human body, whole or in parts, and the driftwood of the wrecks, pretty well covers the water – and stew them all up together in a narrow harbour, and you will have a tolerable imitation of the real essence of Balaklava. If this is not piquante enough, let some men be instructed to sit and smoke on the powder-barrels landing on the quay; which I myself saw two men doing to-day, on the Ordnance Wharf.

Monday, December 4th. – The *"Europa,"* steam-ship, came in this afternoon with draughts, and the 97th regiment – 1100 men in all. Last night the Russians from Kamara made an attempt to get into the town and fire the shipping. They were intercepted, – some shot, and some taken prisoners. It was well they were; for had they not been, Balaklava by this time would have existed only in the past tense, as I should also have done most probably myself – an event on which I do not wish to calculate just yet.
There are Russian residents permitted in Balaklava; amongst them a Mr. Upton, son of the engineer who constructed the forts of Sebastopol, and who was taken prisoner when we first marched down upon that place.

Thursday, December 7th. – The *"Queen of the South"* came in to-day with Turks on board, but was sent on to Eupatoria to disembark them. The *"Sydney"* also arrived with part of the 34th on board, and Mr. Chenery, the Times correspondent at Constantinople. Several men dined on board, and we had no lack of intelligent conversation for that evening at least, whatever the case may usually be.
Captain Hillyar, of the *"Agamemnon,"* came down from the trenches to-day and called on me. He tells me the French were repulsed last night in attacking a Russian battery; and also that the Russians made a sortie on our trenches, from which we drove them back. It appears that the Russians are every day improving their position, as far as new batteries, new trenches, and fresh guns go. A story is current in Balaklava (but people in Balaklava are apt to be scandalous) that one of the Engineers, whose business it indubitably is to watch the various points of attack, being in a battery this morning (whose battery I will not mention), a new mud fort, with sixteen guns mounted and in position, was pointed out to him. *"God bless my soul; so there is! I never knew anything about that!"* was his exclamation. A Maltese man and a woman were found murdered on the rocks just outside Balaklava yesterday. I have not heard that anything has been done towards tracing the crime; indeed, such a process would be impossible in such a crowd and confusion of all nations, languages, and peoples.

Sunday, December 10th. – A mild, warm, damp day. I write so seldom in my journal now, because I have nothing to say, except to grieve over the cruel detention of the mail, now four days over-due.

Tuesday, 12th. – Heavy firing last night from nine o'clock till twelve – followed this morning by an exquisite specimen of Balaklava reports. They said, *"The Russians had come down last night in force, and had established themselves (or endeavoured to do so, I forget which) between the army in front and the army in the rear; that the Rifles had fired away all their ammunition; and that the Russian loss was (as usual) tremendous!"* An Artillery officer, who came down this evening from the trenches, in which he had passed all the previous night, was considerably astonished to hear of this wondrous battle; but said that the Rifles certainly fancied they heard the sound of approaching troops, and blazed away as hard as they could – firing all their ammunition; – the result being, I believe, one dead Russian!

Saturday, December 16th. – Torrents of rain have fallen. The country is more swampy than any words of mine can convey an idea of. Fresh Russian reinforcements have arrived, both to the army in Sebastopol and the army in the field. To-day two steamers arrived; one full of Artillery, and the other with the 89th regiment on board. The French have been landing troops very fast, the last few days, at Kherson; and there is a sort of vague idea floating about in the minds of men that a battle is in meditation on the 19th.

The French, who the other day put their admirable walking ambulance at our disposal to bring down our 1300 sick, have to-day lent us sixty horses to assist to drag up the munitions de guerre. Finding it impossible, by any amount of curses and blows, to get as much strength out of a dying horse as out of one in full vigour, they have at last agreed to give up the attempt; and 400 Turks are to be stationed on the hills to unload the carts at the bottom, and load them again at the top, passing their shot and shell up from hand to hand. A few Russian prisoners are also employed in assisting the French to mend our roads. Their countenances are wonderfully alike, all with flat noses and short chins; but they seem cheerful and wondrously willing to work. I hear they receive one shilling a-day, and a ration of rum.

Sunday, 17th. – Went to morning church; afterwards walked with Mr. Anderson, and, returning through a deluge of mud, met the 89th and 17th regiments, which had disembarked at an hour's notice, as an attack is expected to-morrow, it being St. Nicholas's day, when the Russian soldiers are supposed to have an extra ration of rakee; and as they never fight unless half drunk, the argument is not so bad after all.

Monday, 18th. – A brilliant, warm day tempted us out; and, at eleven o'clock, Henry, Mr. Rochfort, Mr. Aspinall, and I, found ourselves on horseback starting for the Monastery of St. George. After about three miles of extremely heavy riding, we got upon the downs, and broke our wearisome walking-pace.

The monastery soon came in sight. Built on the edge of a rock, with a precipitous and wooded descent to the sea, it stands quite alone, a solid and rather fine building, surrounded by massive rocks and high cliffs.

We tied our horses to the railings of a church outside the precincts, and, guided by a Zouave, penetrated to the gardens within. A few monks were amusing themselves on the terraces, and against the rails, over which we leaned to take in the beauty of the abrupt cliffs, which sloped, laden with trees and foliage even at this time of year, down to the water's edge. Mr. Rochfort left us, and presently returned with a handful of Russian stocks in bloom, which he gave to me. Several Russian families have taken refuge here from the lines of the English and French armies. One Englishman interested us all; a Mr. Willis, who had been for five-and-thirty years head caulker in the harbour of Sebastopol. He grumbled sorely at the advent of his countrymen, who, as he said, had pulled down his house, and loop-holed it, and had destroyed his vineyard – his 999 trees!

General Bosquet and staff rode up as we left, and several English officers were leaving at the same time as ourselves. We had a cheery canter home, during which one of us put up a hare, which, although we had a very speedy greyhound with us, we could not catch. I rode the white Spanish horse.

Tuesday, 19th. – Rode my dear old horse to-day, for the first time since his starvation, and nearly cried with joy as I felt him straining on the bit. A few days ago, when he came down from the front, a mere skinful of bones, and with an expression of human woe and suffering in his large sad eyes, he haunted me night and day; but, remembering my former loss, I would neither mention him in this book, nor would I inquire whether he was dead or alive, as each morning came, and to-day he was able to canter for a couple of dozen yards.

Wednesday, 20th. – Rode the white Spanish horse, and hearing that the French were intending to make a reconnaissance, we cantered into the plain and joined them. The Chasseurs d'Afrique, the 6ième Dragons, and another regiment (which, I do not know) were riding towards Kamara and Canrobert's Hill.

As they approached the latter, the enemy showed themselves on the top; mutual skirmishers were sent out; several shots were fired. One Dragon was killed, a Chasseur wounded, and a Chasseur horse destroyed; and then, after sitting and looking at each other for some little time, we turned and rode slowly back.

The object of this reconnaissance was to endeavour to ascertain the number of the enemy, and also to try to recover the batteries abandoned by the Turks on the 25th of October. Whether either of these objects was accomplished, I cannot tell, but I think not. It seemed to me cruel enough to leave the one poor fellow in the middle of the great plain, lying on his face, in his gay-coloured uniform, to be either prodded to death with the Cossack lances, or eaten by the eagles and the wild dogs. The scene haunted me for days – aye, even in my dreams.

Friday, 22nd. – Incessant rain.

Saturday, 23rd. – Ditto, only twice as hard.

Sunday, 24th. – The two previous days condensed in one; and this is Christmas eve. How many hearts in our sodden camp must feel sad and lonely to-day! How many pictures of home, and how many faces (how much loved we never knew till now) rise before our hearts, all beaming with a happiness probably unpossessed by them, but in which our imagination loves to clothe them! Alas! how many assembled round the blazing fires at home drink no healths, but meet in sorrow to pour out the wassail as a libation to the many honoured dead! Heavy firing to-day from the ships. Sir Edmund Lyons has been but three days in command. He is popular, and much is expected of him.

Christmas Day. – A brilliant frosty morning. After church Henry and I walked up to the Cavalry camp, and invited Lord Killeen and Colonel De Salis to join our dinner party on board the *"Star of the South,"* which somehow was prolonged far into the night.

Wednesday, 27th. – We started intending to ride up to head quarters, but the roads were so deep and rotten, so full of holes that seemed to have no bottom, the day was so raw, and our progress so slow, that, notwithstanding my endeavours to keep my habit short and temper long, I was too much disgusted and wearied to struggle further than our Cavalry camp. The cold to-night is intense, and as we have no fire on board this ship our sufferings are very great. But *"there is in every depth a lower still,"* and we should be worse off in the trenches. It is when suffering from these minor evils of cold and hunger (for our table is very much neglected), that I feel most how much my patience, endurance, and fortitude are tried. The want of fire, of a carpet, of even a chair, makes itself terribly felt just now.

Friday, 29th. – Lieutenant Ross, of the *"Stromboli,"* called on me this afternoon, and joined us in a charming walk to the ruins of the Genoese Fort, whence we watched the sparkling sunlight on the sea; and then turning to our left, we stretched across the hills to the Marine and Rifle camp, and returned by descending the precipitous cliff into Balaklava.

Saturday, 30th. – The French Cavalry, a regiment of Zouaves, and some of the Highlanders of Sir Colin Campbell's division, made a reconnaissance to-day over the ground supposed to have been occupied by the Russian army under Liprandi. This force they found had almost entirely vacated the plain, owing, as we suppose, to the severe weather cutting off their supplies of provisions. The French set fire to all the huts they found, and the party returned about dusk, having met with very few casualties.
I did not go out with the reconnaissance, as our horses require rest rather than work, and would never have carried us through the deep mud for so many hours. Instead, we walked up to the camp, where the sale of the late Major Oldham's kit was in progress. We were fortunate enough to find some excellent soup, manufactured by Captain Jennings, of the 13th Light Dragoons, of which I am afraid we left him very little. We hear that Lord George Paget has started on his return to the Crimea.

Monday, January 1st, 1855. – Day cruelly cold, but very bright. Henry and I walked to the Genoese Fort, and watched the ships sailing harbourwards on the calm and shining sea. The 39th regiment arrived in the *"Golden Fleece,"* and Mr. Foster shortly after came on board the *"Star of the South;"* and we discussed the merry old days spent together at Weymouth, until the sound of the old waltzes rang in my ears, and the horn of Mr. Farquharson's huntsman came up echoing from far over the sea.

Wednesday, January 3rd. – The quay covered with French soldiers, whom I watched with the greatest amusement, as they absolutely plundered our shot and shell, so rapidly did it disappear under their hands for conveyance to the front. Before our men can collect their wits for the work, 100, 200, 250 shell are passing from hand to hand into the waggons waiting to receive them. But, as their officer remarked to me, *"Les Anglais sont de très bons soldats, mais ils ne savent pas faire la guerre. Ils se battent très bien (Allons, mes enfans, vite! vite!), mais ils n'aiment pas travailler. Ils ont peur de se souiller les mains. (Nous voilà prêts pour le départ.) Nous sommes aussi prêts pour aller à Sevastopol; mais les Anglais – c'est eux qui nous font toujours – attendre – attendre. Madame, j'ai l'honneur de vous saluer,"* and away went the whole corps, every two men carrying a 10-inch shell. Ah, how have our resources been wasted! – our horses killed! – our men invalided; while over it all broods the most culpable indifference!

Tuesday, January 9th. – A day of miraculous escape. Henry and I were writing in the cabin, and I was just finishing a note which a sergeant of the 62nd was waiting to take up to the front – our ship had been engaged for some days previous in taking in powder and ammunition, and she had on board nearly 1000 tons – when suddenly the sergeant put his head in at the door, and asked if the note were ready.
I said, *"Not yet; you must wait a moment."* The reply was, *"I cannot wait – for – the ship's on fire!"* A moment after, and the noise and hurry showed us it was too true. The fire was in the lower hold, and burning within six feet of the magazine! At such a time there was no thought of fear. It had been raining; and Henry and I, unwilling to add to the crowd forward, after getting some galoshes, went on deck.
We were then advised to go and stand on shore, and to take my poor maid, who was screaming, and praying to every saint in the calendar, by turns. We were soon overboard, and watching the exertions of the men at the pumps. The hose of the steam-ship *"Niagara"* was in a few moments at work, as well as our own, and in a short time the alarm was over, and the fire extinguished. Moored next us was the *"Earl of Shaftesbury,"* also a powder ship; and a little a-head of us lay the *"Medora,"* likewise with powder on board.
All felt that their last moment was come; and yet, a strange exultation possessed my heart in contemplating so magnificent a death – to die with hundreds in so stupendous an explosion, which would not only have destroyed every vessel in harbour, and the very town itself, but would have altered the whole shape of the bay, and the echoes of which would have rung through the world!

Wednesday, January 10th. – Not liking the anchorage, after yesterday's experience, I endeavoured to ride up to head quarters, to petition for rooms on shore, but the heavy rain stopped all that.

Saturday, 13th. – Frost, snow, and bitter cold. This morning I ran up on deck, for the day was bright and sunny, in spite of the cold, keen air. It was a wondrous sight! – everything buried in a foot of snow; rocks, houses, gun-limbers, plants, and tents, all covered. The ships in harbour were the prettiest: they were all dressed in purest white; the capstan tops looking like huge twelfth cakes; the yards and spars glittering like rods of ice bound together by fairy ropes of snow; the whole glistening in the sunlight like an illumination.
I thank God heartily that I can see and appreciate beauty of every kind. How many have eyes which see not; ears which ear not; hearts which cannot understand! – men who perpetually remind one of the character described by Wordsworth, of whom he says – *"The primrose by the river's brim A yellow primrose was to him, And it was nothing more."*

Monday, 15th. – Took the dear old horse's bridle over my arm, and walked him up to camp, as he has not been out for some days, and it is too slippery to ride. Appreciated most gratefully the kindness of Captain Naylor, who sent me out, two days ago, a wondrous plaid, the thickness and warmth of which is of the greatest service to me. Tried to find a pair of muffetees for poor Lord Killeen, whose fingers, like mine, are chilled to the bone.

Tuesday, January 16th. – We changed our anchorage to-day, and moved to a berth nearer the mouth of the harbour. Ingress and egress to the ship is now much more difficult, as we are much further from shore.
Thus we shall lose many of our most frequent visitors, and be made almost prisoners on board the ship, which is a nuisance that we resent in true English fashion, by grumbling all day long. A large augmentation of the Russian army arrived yesterday near Inkermann. Our (English) force consists now of 11,000 bayonets. The leaders of the Times have, I see, taken up the subject warmly enough, and by so doing have cheered and refreshed many a heart that was well nigh tired of *"The trouble and the pain of living."*
Friday, 19th. – Captain Sayer, who has been so long a resident on board the *"Star of the South,"* left us early and suddenly this morning, fearing he should not be able to reach England by the expiration of his leave. When going ashore this afternoon, I discovered that, not satisfied with the ten dead horses and three camels already rotting on the shore, they make a practice of goading all the dying commissariat animals to this corner, to add to the congregation already assembled.

Saturday, 20th. – For two days we have had alongside our ship a Turkish steamer, so close as to chafe our ship's side very considerably. She took up a position in the harbour pointed out to her by the authorities; and soon after she had anchored, she began blowing off her steam, and emptying the burning cinders overboard between her own side and ours. Henry and Captain Frain were both on deck; but it was not until after many and frantic efforts that they at last made the captain of the steamer understand that we had powder on board. To-day 360 plague-stricken Turks have been put into her; but one becomes so indifferent and callous that nothing dismays one now. Henry and I tried to go out fishing this morning, but we got the net foul of the rocks, and caught nothing. The band of the 14th regiment was playing on board the *"Emeu"* all the time.

They have just arrived in harbour. The 39th, on board the *"Golden Fleece,"* are suffering terribly from sickness, and have lost so many men that a portion of them are to be disembarked and sent ashore to-day, so as to render her less crowded and more fit for the accommodation of the sick.

The *"Arabia,"* steam-ship, which succeeded the Turkish steamer in the occupation of the berth alongside us, was discovered to be very extensively on fire this morning about five o'clock. I look upon the preservation of our lives, entrusted as they are to such inefficient and unprincipled hands as those who have the management of ships in this harbour, to be a perpetual miracle.

Wednesday, 24th. – Riding to the camp to-day I met Lord Raglan coming down to Balaklava, and I took the opportunity of asking his lordship whether I might not live in any house, however small, on shore. My request was not acceded to.

Saturday, 27th. – 250 sick embarked to-day.

Sunday, 28th. – 130 sick embarked to-day.

Monday, 29th. – 295 sick embarked to-day. Truly our army is in a lamentable state. I have grieved until I have no power of grieving left. I think that if I knew I was going to die myself, I should merely shrug my shoulders and lie down quietly. We have no ambulance waggons; they are nearly all broken down, or the mules are dead, or the drivers are dead or dead drunk: as well one as the other, as far as usefulness goes.

Our poor Cavalry horses, as we know full well, are all unequal to the task of carrying down the sick; and the French have provided transports for us for some time. They were complaisant enough about it at first, but now (the men I mean) begin to grumble, and to do their work cruelly. One poor fellow, wounded and frostbitten in the hands and feet, was taken roughly from his mule and huddled down in the mud, despite his agonised screams and cries. Another Frenchman drove his empty mule so carelessly past one that was still laden as to cut the poor sufferer's legs with the iron bar, and cause him cruel pain. Why can we not tend our own sick? Why are we so helpless and so broken down? Oh, England! England! blot out the lion and the unicorn: let the supporters of your arms henceforth be, Imbecility and Death! A cargo of *"navvies"* came out to-day in the *"Lady Alice Lambton."* Their arrival makes a great sensation. Some of them immediately went ashore, and set out for a walk *"to see if they could see e'er a — Roosshian."* The 39th, who have been hitherto employed as working parties on the road, yield their work to the navvies, after having given the greatest satisfaction at it themselves. Henry and I dined in camp with Captain Portal, of the 4th Light Dragoons, who gave us a dinner that contrasted wonderfully with our hard fare on board ship, and whose hospitable and cheerful welcome we shall always remember with pleasure.

Tuesday, 30th. – Captain Hillyar, who came in last night in the *"Malacca,"* called on me this morning with his brother, and asked us to dinner to-night.

Wednesday, 31st. – Eight nurses, under the direction of a *"Lady Eldress"* and Miss Shaw Stewart, came up to-day from Scutari to the Balaklava hospital. We lunched on board the *"Malacca,"* and met Captain Lushington, who engaged us to luncheon on Tuesday next. The report is that the Grand Dukes are again in Sebastopol.

Monday, February 5th. – Dined with Major Peel. Oh! what terrible work it is to ride over these wretched roads! You flounder along in the most helpless manner; and coming back in the dark, I put the reins on the old horse's neck, and exhorted him in this wise: – *"Remember, 'Bob,' that any fool of a horse can tumble down here, so pray recollect what a much cleverer horse you are than any other of your species."* I conclude the admonition had the desired effect; at any rate, we got safely home.

Tuesday, 6th. – A beautiful morning, but blowing very heavily. We started about twelve for the naval camp, and ten minutes after down came the rain! We persevered, and arriving at last like drowned rats, were most hospitably entertained. Captain Lushington appeared sufficiently amused at my determined indifference to the rain. The weather cleared about four; and we had a delightful ride home along the high land, and then down to Kadekoi, by the brook in the valley, and over the dykes. I hardly know whose heart laughed the most, the brave old horse's or mine, as he laid his slender ears back, and, bearing on the bit, flung himself along, as though the starvation and the cruel suffering were all a myth, and he was once more in the merry hunting field at home.

Thursday, 8th. – Roused in the middle of the night by a report that the Russians were coming down in force, and that the crews of the transports must all turn out armed. What an order! What could such a disorganised rabble do in the midst of regular troops? They would most probably fire away at whatever came first, and cause endless worry and confusion.

Saturday, 10th. – Exchanged the *"Star of the South"* for the *"Herefordshire,"* a fine old East Indiaman, and a most comfortable ship; a most desirable change in every way as far as comfort and good living go.

Monday, 12th. – What a soft and pleasant day. The sun was so hot as to make it impossible to walk uphill. We sat in the valley and thoroughly enjoyed the genial day, and, then descending to the shore, watched the varying colours on the rocks and sea. At night came on a hurricane of wind and rain.

Tuesday, 13th. – Blowing terrific squalls. Captain Lushington, however, came on board, at great risk, to call on me. Some of the sick officers, who are on board the *"Herefordshire,"* left to-day for Scutari, and others came in their places. Amongst them Colonel D——, of the 90th, who had wounded himself this morning while playing with a revolver.

Friday, 16th. – Henry, Mr. Foster, Mr. Carr, Captain Lushington, and I rode over to the monastery, and I was as much pleased with it the second time of seeing it as the first. They report an attack on Inkermann this morning, but, although the firing was very heavy, I believe nothing extraordinary occurred. Lord Lucan sailed for England to-day.

Tuesday, 20th. – A reconnaissance in force started this morning at four o'clock, to endeavour to surprise and take the outlying army over the hills. The snow began to fall immediately that the men were under arms, and presently came down with such hearty good-will as to render it impossible to proceed The English Infantry who turned out were the 14th, 17th, 42nd, 71st, 79th, 93rd. The Light Cavalry, also, made a contribution of about thirty-five or thirty-eight men and horses. But after groping about in the intense cold and utter darkness, till every man was saturated and chilled to the bone, they were all ordered to turn in again.
On board our ship, the *"Herefordshire,"* we have a most painful scene. One of the chaplains (Mr. Wyatt), who has long been ill of fever, is now delirious and in the utmost danger. He lies in a cabin separated from us by only a Venetian shutter; his incoherent ravings and frantic efforts to escape intrude themselves above the hushed voices of all who occupy the cabin. Fortunately, we none of us have a dread of infection. Poor Mr. Taylor, too, another chaplain, whose exertions have been most unremitting and most noble, lies also on board another ship in the shadow of death. I know that Mr. Taylor has spent day after day in these pestilential hospitals, never giving himself rest or purer air.

Saturday, 24th. – Lunched in camp with Colonel Doherty, and afterwards went to see one of the women of our regiment, who is suffering from fever. I found her lying on a bed on the wet ground; she had lain there, in cold and rain, wind and snow, for twelve days. By her side, in the wet mud, was a piece of ration biscuit, a piece of salt pork, some cheese, and a tin pot with some rum! Nice fever diet! She, having failed to make herself popular among the women during her health, was left by them when she was sick; and not a soul had offered to assist the poor helpless, half-delirious creature, except her husband, and a former mate of his when he was a sailor.

Thursday, March 1st. -It being reported that all the transports are to be ordered out of Balaklava harbour, Captain Lushington rode down from the Naval Brigade, and most kindly, and with great consideration, offered to put up a hut for us in the camp – it being too cold for me to think of living in a tent. Captain Lushington, who is a very old friend of Henry's family, could not have given them a greater proof of friendship: he has offered to furnish men to put up the hut, dig the cooking-house, stables, &c.

Sunday, March 4th. – The *"Herefordshire,"* which Admiral Boxer had long been threatening, was duly turned out of Balaklava harbour at eight o'clock this morning. We had been cried *"wolf"* to so often, that when the order really did arrive it took us all by surprise. The hurry and confusion was most absurd; and, after all, we were obliged to go out to sea in her, and return in the tug.
But it was a lovely day, and we enjoyed the sail. Every one left the *"Herefordshire"* with regret; and we took leave of kind, cordial, hospitable Captain Stevenson with many expressions of hope that we should soon meet again.
We returned to the *"Star of the South."*

Monday, 5th. – Started on horseback at one o'clock, to attend the *"First Spring Meeting,"* the first race of the season. Wonderful, that men who have been starved with cold and hunger, drowned in rain and mud, wounded in action, and torn with sickness,. should on the third warm, balmy day start into fresh life like butterflies, and be as eager and fresh for the rare old English sport, as if they were in the ring at Newmarket, or watching the colours coming round *"the corner."*
There were four races: the first I was not in time to see.
Just as the riders were going to the starting-post for the second race, somebody called out, *"The picquets are coming in; the Russians must be advancing!"* Away we all hurried to the camp, but found out it was a false alarm, caused by two Russian deserters whom our picquet had taken. It did not take long to return to the race-ground: and the transition struck me as equally abrupt – from the race-course to the battle-field, from the camp to the course. Two pony races were won by sheer good riding, by Captain Thomas, R. H. A.; and after the *"Consolation Stakes,"* as the sun was still high, the meeting dispersed for a dog-hunt.
I rode with them as far as Karani, and then turned back. I could not join in or countenance in any way a sport that appears to me so unsportsmanlike, so cruel, so contrary to all good feeling, as hunting a dog.
I must mention that our hut progresses wonderfully; it is nearly finished, and the carpenters are making me a table. We are indebted to the kindness of Captain Franklyn, master of the *"Columba,"* for a large sheet of plate glass, which makes a magnificent window.

Tuesday, 6th. – The *"Canadian"* went down to Constantinople to-day full of sick. What a serene and balmy day!

Wednesday, 7th. – In spite of a fog, which hung like a pall over the summits of the hills, I resolved to join a riding party we had made to the Monastery of St. George.
I thought that I could fight with a Crimean fog, and get the best of it; but I very soon found out my mistake. Oh, the fever, lassitude, aches, and pains of this evening!

Wednesday, 14th. – The warm sun drew me out of the cheerless cabin, and tempted me to try and walk on deck, though so weak as to be unable to do so without help.

Thursday, 15th. – A brilliant day for our Second Meeting. The horses are improving wonderfully; and in the hurdle race for English horses which had wintered in the Crimea, they went at the fences as if they liked the fun. Men of every regiment, English and French, were on the course. Amongst the latter, a Comte Bertrand, who amused me by the eloquence with which he descanted on his own powers of equitation, his *"hotel"* in the country, his ten English horses, and English coachman called *"Johnson."* He spent the evening on board the *"Star of the South,"* and showed us that, whatever his equestrianism might be, he could play at ecarté.

Sunday, 18th. – Walked up to camp with Colonel Somerset and Mr. Foster; found the house so far advanced that we settled to come into it on Tuesday. Nothing reaches us from the front, except reports that the French attack, and fail nightly in taking, the rifle-pits of the Russians.
The French can beat us in their commissariat and general management, but the Englishman retains his wondrous power of fighting that nothing can rob him of but death.

▲ Officers and men of the 8th Hussars. We think that Captain Henry Duberly was the fourth from left.

▲ Lieutenant-Colonel (later Lieutenant-General) James Brudenell, 7th Earl of Cardigan, on 'Ronald', c1854 Oil on millboard by Alfred Frank de Prades. Cardigan born the 16 October 1797 and died the 28 March 1868), was an officer in the British Army who commanded the Light Brigade during the Crimean War. He led the Charge of the Light Brigade at the Battle of Balaclava. Throughout his life in politics and his long military career he characterised the arrogant and extravagant aristocrat of the period. His progression through the Army was marked by many episodes of extraordinary incompetence, but this can be measured against his generosity to the men under his command and genuine bravery. As a member of the landed aristocracy he had actively and steadfastly opposed any political reform in Britain, but in the last year of his life he relented and came to acknowledge that such reform would bring benefit to all classes of society.

CHAPTER V

❖

THE
CAMP

▲ Colonel Frederick G. Shewell, full-length portrait, seated on horseback, facing left. C.B., commanding Hussar Brigade.
Photo by Roger Fenton

THE CAMP

"Three hosts combine to offer sacrifice
Three tongues prefer strange orisons on high,
Three gaudy standards flout the pale blue sky."

Byron

*T*UESDAY, *March,* 20th. – Left the *"Star of the South,"* and once more resumed our life in camp. A gleaming day, with lovely lights and shadows. Thanks to the kindness of Captain Buckley, of the Scots' Fusileer Guards, and Colonel Somerset, who lent us means of conveyance for our *"impedimenta,"* I was able to move up in one day. Major Peel and Captain Cook, of the 11th Hussars, saved us from starving by most hospitably inviting us to dine. The dinner was enlivened by a perfect storm of musketry, which made us fancy something unusual was going on in front; but perhaps my being unaccustomed to be disturbed by musketry at night makes me fancy it worse than it is. I am writing at one o'clock, and am, oh, so tired!

Wednesday, March 21st. – In our saddles by half-past ten, riding towards Kamiesh. We were to have been joined by Colonel Somerset, who kindly undertook to be our guide; but by some fatality we missed him, and reached Kamiesh at last by a very circuitous route. Here we made purchases of chickens, carrots, petits pois verts, and various other necessaries of life; all of which we packed upon our saddles, and then cantered home. Henry decorated the pommel of his saddle with six fowls, slung three on each side, and *"Bob,"* who had never been turned into a market-horse before, was alike frightened at their screams, and disgusted at the way they scratched him with their claws; so he wisely took the shortest and quickest way home, hardly breaking from his hand gallop the whole way. Poor chickens!

Thursday, 22nd. – The chickens are all walking about as if nothing had happened, except that one or two go a little stiff. Colonel Shewell, Lord Killeen, Colonel Doherty, Major Peel, and Captain Cook called on me to-day. The French took, and held, four rifle-pits last night, which accounts for the tremendous firing that shook the hut. We hear that the loss was very great: they report here, 300 French, and eight English officers, names at present unknown.

Friday, March 23rd. – Our 93rd battery firing this morning, we ran to see what was the cause. A shell burst just at the foot of Canrobert's Hill; and with our glasses we saw two deserters running in, while three or four of our men went to meet them. Lord George Paget and Colonel Douglas called on us to-day.
The former has promised to give me a little smooth terrier. The establishment only wants a dog to be complete; and I, who have never before been without a dog, look forward with great pleasure to having this little terrier to make a pet of.

Saturday, 24th. – Can this be a journal of a campaign? I think I must change its name to a new edition of the *"Racing Calendar."* The French races to-day were very amusing. The course was crowded, the sun shone, and French officers *were riding at full gallop everywhere, and making their horses go through all the tricks of the manege. The "steeple-chase"* course, *"avec huit obstacles,"* was delightful: the hurdles were not sufficiently high to puzzle an intelligent and active poodle; the ditches were like the trenches in a celery bed; and the wall about two feet and a half high. But it was a very merry meeting.
We rode up with Captain Lushington, Colonel Douglas, Colonel Somerset, Mr. Vansittart, and Major Peel, and afterwards lunched with le Comte Bertrand, on game pie and champagne.

Sunday, 25th. – A day reminding one of the great heats in Bulgaria. The men fell out in all directions from church parade. Late in the afternoon Henry and I rode up to hear the band of the 27ième de la ligne.

▲ View from hill of cavalry camp showing people, horses, and tents on the plains of Balaklava. Fenton's image

Monday, 26th. – Races at the Fourth Division; chiefly remarkable for the difference between the Englishman's and Frenchman's idea of a fence. To-day we had a formidable wall of four foot, built as firmly as possible, while the ground on either side was hard enough to make it anything but a tempting jump.

Wednesday, March 28th. – More races. Count Bertrand, Mr. Foster, Captain Lushington, Colonel Somerset, and Mr. Vansittart came to luncheon, and we rode afterwards to the course. *"Goodboy,"* ridden by Captain Thomas, came in an easy winner. The day was most lovely, but too hot for enjoyment.
We fancied that summer was come, and that we had done with the cold weather.

Saturday, 31st. – Winter has returned. The very hills are blue with cold. A hard, frozen-looking haze covers the landscape, whilst a cruel north-east wind searches one throughout, filling the bones with rheumatism, and the lungs with cold. I did not move from my stove till evening, when we were engaged to dine with Major Peel. We did not return until rather late, which was fortunate, as, hearing groans coming from the stable as we passed, Henry went to see what was the matter, and found that my chestnut horse had had a kicking fit on him, and had kicked away at the principal post till he brought the whole roof, rafters and all, down about his ears. The weight fell on all the horses' backs, but chiefly on the poor pony, *"Whisker,"* who was supporting all the heaviest rafters, and groaning with disgust Luckily, none of the horses were hurt.

Tuesday, April 3rd. – Went over with a large party to Kamiesh. We hear it is the general opinion that the fire on Sebastopol will recommence in a few days. The number of guns that it is supposed will be at work on that day, English, French, and Russian, are computed at between 1600 and 1700. Meanwhile our hut is shaken every night by the explosions of the heavy guns, and we ourselves are roused by the incessant rain of musketry. Some few are sanguine as to the result of this bombardment. I heard one person assert that in his opinion the place could not stand twenty-four hours against such a fire.

The ships are to make a demonstration, as though they were going to attack the forts on the North side, but it is doubtful whether they will attack. War, horrid war! Why can we not ride in peace over this lovely country, abounding in flowers and coloured with tints, which, by their freshness and beauty, remind me perpetually of Copley Fielding's pictures. It is strange that, to express my admiration for nature, I am obliged to compare it with art; but I never saw elsewhere scenery so clear, so wondrously coloured, looking so warm, yet actually so cold. It impresses me as a picture would. I admire it, but it does not affect me. Perhaps the absence of trees takes away from the "home" feeling; and, by making the landscape appear like a picture, fails to excite any sympathetic feelings of admiration. The scenery and I may get on better when these cruel cold winds have passed, and the glorious sun throws some of his magnificent heat into it.

Saturday, 7th. – Light Division races. The day was perfect; the races well attended; and, had it not been for an accident, the sight of which seemed to stun me, and stop every pulse in my body, we should have had an enjoyable day. In the steeple-chase course they had built a wall, over four foot, and as firm as it could be built, turfed over at the top, and as solid as an alderman's wit. Captain Thomas, R. H. A., and Captain Shiffner, two of our best riders, were in the race. The crowd collected round the wall to see the jump, and I shoved my horse in as close as I could. After a moment's suspense, they are off – three noble horses, all well ridden. Mr. Wilkins's horse takes the wall easily, and rushes on; Captain Shiffner's horse strikes it with his chest, and, after one effort, rolls over headlong, falling on his rider; Captain Thomas's horse clears the wall, but lands on the man and horse already down. At first, neither was supposed to have survived; but at last Captain Thomas moved, and presently they found that poor Captain Shiffner was not dead; but the doctors pronounced him so much injured internally as to leave no hope of his surviving the night.

They were both carried from the ground. About an hour after we rode to inquire for Captain Thomas, who was lying in a hut close by, and found that he was conscious. His first words were, *"Who won the race?"* Of poor Captain Shiffner we hear there is no hope.

I think this has rather made me lose my liking for steeple-chasing.

Sunday, 8th. – I heard this morning that poor Captain Shiffner died during the night. What little comfort for the mourners at home to reflect that his life was lost in such a way! – with neither glory nor honour to assuage the bitterness of death. Such an accident, coming in the midst of strong excitement, seems to make a pause, a stillness, in one's own life. I am so shocked, so nervous by what I have seen, that I am fit for nothing; and yet, if he had been shot in the trenches, he would have had, most probably, no other requiem than, *"Poor Shiffner was killed last night." "Dear me! was he? Poor fellow!"* instead of forming the subject for thought and conversation to all.

Six o'clock. – Colonel Somerset has just called, and tells me the report of Shiffner's death is false; that he lives, and they have hopes of him.

Monday, 9th. – Torrents of rain; incessant, soaking, unrelenting rain, in the midst of which the roar of the sullen guns came down to us with a sort of muffled sound; and no wonder, coming through so dense and sodden an atmosphere. Of course, everybody who was not absolutely on duty in the trenches staid at home, except, I believe, one or two soldiers, too red hot to be affected by the rain. We hear that our opening fire took the Russians so much by surprise, that each of our guns fired seven rounds before they returned a single shot. The report is (as usual) that our fire is doing great damage to the enemy's works; but we hear that always, as a matter of course.

Tuesday, 10th. – Rode up ourselves to the front to watch the firing. We saw it to great advantage (it being a very clear day) from a point opposite to Sir Richard England's division. I have not been to the front for some time; not, at least, far enough to observe the works before the town; they therefore strike me as being about twice as extended as when I saw them last, in, I think, December. The Mamelon and Malakoff batteries, both new, have opened a most formidable fire; while the Redan appears, to my eyes, much better furnished with guns in and about it than before. We did not remain long in the Quarry, but went to the Mortar Battery, on our right, to watch the practice of the Sea-service mortars. Somehow I never felt less interested in any transaction of the war. I cannot believe that this bombardment will be productive of the slightest effect on a position which we have allowed to become so strong. When Sir Richard England asked me, whilst we were watching from the Quarries, whether I was interested, I gave him two answers, equally truthful – *"Yes,"* and *"No."* If we could see any point on which to build a hope – any gun dismounted – any embrasure knocked in, we could find something upon which to fasten and feed an interest; but it seems to me very like a bombardment in a picture – blue sky overhead, a town, and innumerable puffs of smoke all round it.

Wednesday, 11th. – Rode up again, but this time to the French left attack, and took up our position near the *Maison d'Eau.* I was much pleased by obtaining a better view of the town than I had hitherto been able to discover. We were almost over the harbour. We saw steamers and little boats pulling between the forts.
We saw people moving in the town. The sea and the sky, all God's part of the picture, looked so blue and calm; while all man's part of the picture was noise, smoke, and confusion. I could not but reflect, though perhaps such thoughts are inappropriate here, upon the vastness of that Rest, which enwraps, as with an infinite mantle, all the fretfulness and vain effort of this world; and I must confess, that instead of attending to the statistics of my companions, I lost myself in a wondrous reverie, inspired by the contrasts of the scene before me, on that most blessed of all theories – *"There remaineth, therefore, a rest."*

Sunday, 15th. – Captain Lushington called, and seemed in despair. It appears that his batter had knocked a breach in some particular spot at which they had been hammering with that wonderful energy and inconceivably careless courage which has characterised them so especially throughout the war, and had made an opening sufficiently wide for troops to storm, but *"the French were not ready."* Captain Lushington's brigade has suffered severely during this last bombardment, both in guns and men; above a hundred of the latter are killed and wounded. We endeavoured to *"administer to the mind diseased"* a little of the tonic wherewith we have often refreshed ourselves during the last twelvemonth, and which we have found most serviceable. It is composed chiefly of one ingredient – namely, the contents of an old proverb: – *"Blessed are they who expect nothing, for they will not be disappointed."* Leaving Captain Lushington to try the efficacy of my cure, Henry and I rode up to the French band playing on the hill.

Tuesday, 17th. – Put up a large Turkish tent outside the hut, to serve as a drawing-room, and later as a dining-room; for we find it inconvenient to have only a room of twelve foot square in which to eat, sleep, and receive company. This tent, large, hexagonal, double lined with dark blue, and open at both ends, is a great addition to one's comfort. We have it matted, carpetted, and furnished with a table and an armchair – luxuries which were to us, when in Bulgaria, but a dream of our youth. There is a great stir in Balaklava, owing to the arrival and disembarkation of the 10th Hussars, who have come from India, and are reported to be 680 strong, and mounted on the finest Arabs in the world (at least, so says Colonel Parlby, who commands them).
Every one is anxious to see this new regiment; and it is most amusing to hear the various speculations regarding these same horses – some declaring that there is nothing like an Arab horse; he is up to any weight, can endure any fatigue, live without food, and never sleeps: whereas others remember the mud of last winter, and how the vast thews and sinews of the most powerful English horses were only strong enough to pull them into it – and then leave them there to die.

Wednesday, 18th. – We rode up – Henry, Colonel Somerset, Mr. Calvert, and I – to look at such of these *"wondrous winged steeds with manes of gold"* as had landed. We found them perfect in shape, so purely bred that each horse might have been a crowned king; clothed in coats of sheeny satin, that seemed defiant even of the rays of the blessed sun himself when he looked at them; their small heads never resting, and their eyes like outlets for the burning fire within. But I will write down my first impression, and then see if time proves it correct. These horses are not in one respect suited for their work here, and they will fail at the commencement of winter – too small, too light, too excitable. This is merely what strikes me, and I merely write it as a speculation, knowing of this country what I do.

Thursday, April 19th. – A strong reconnaissance went out this morning, commanded by Omar Pasha, to Kamara, to inspect the Russian force, and with the intention of ultimately pushing forward, and allowing the Turks to occupy their old position in the plain from which they ran with such a cheerful alacrity at *"Balaklava."* Omar Pasha is very anxious to impress us favourably with the Turkish force that he has brought with him from Eupatoria, and which is composed of the same men who fought so well at Silistria.

We hear, also, that the soldiers themselves are most anxious to give proof of their courage and steadiness under fire. They assert that the Turks who formed part of our force in the winter were only militia, and not regular troops; and I should fancy that by this time all those poor creatures had died of the plague.

I had arranged to accompany the reconnaissance, but Henry was unfortunately so far from well as to be unable to go, and of course I remained also. I seldom like writing from report; and as I was not present, am unwilling to say anything about this reconnaissance, save that the Russian force appears to be by no means numerous.

Saturday, April 21st. – Rode with Henry and Colonel Poulett Somerset to the head-quarters of the Turkish force, as Omar Pasha had done us the honour to ask us to luncheon. We found him sitting in a small but very light and convenient tent, which opened towards Sebastopol; and being on high ground, we had a very good bird's-eye view of the position of the English and French armies. The band, a remarkably good one, was soon after sent for, and played for some time with a great deal of precision. They played, amongst other morceaux, *"Il Rigoletto,"* and some marches composed by Madame, the wife of Omar Pasha, for His Highness's band. Madame is, I believe, either German or Wallachian, and evidently possesses a knowledge both of the science and esprit de la musique. The pieces played by the band, and written by her, evinced both taste and power.

Luncheon, consisting of champagne and sweetmeats, was going on at the same time as the music; and when both were finished, His Highness ordered his horse, and we accompanied him to General Bosquet's, and afterwards to the brow of a hill opposite the Russian camp, where one of the mountain guns used in the Turkish army was placed and fired, to show General Bosquet its enormous range. These guns are small – made precisely like the barrel of a Minié rifle, about five feet in length, and firing a conical leaden ball of four and a half pounds' weight. It is mounted on a very small carriage, and drawn by a single mule.

Omar Pasha said it would carry 4000 yards. This fact, however, I am unable to vouch for from personal observation, as I never saw the ball after it was put in at the muzzle of the gun – I mean to say, my eyes were too much unaccustomed to follow the shot, nor did we see it strike. But, like true believers, we admitted that it struck wherever we were told it had done so; and, as far as I was concerned, I was quite satisfied.

We then re-mounted, and returned to General Bosquet's tent. Our order of march was somewhat as follows: – Omar Pasha, on a chestnut Arab, which he made go through every evolution that a horse's brain was capable of remembering, or his legs of executing; a group of attendant pashas and effendis, amongst whom we were mixed up; Lieutenant-Colonel Simmonds, English engineer, attached to the Turkish staff; General Bosquet, and one or two French officers belonging to his staff; and an escort of Turkish lancers on small horses, very dirty, very slovenly, and diffusing a fragrance of onions which made one's eyes fill with tears.

We took leave of our host at General Bosquet's camp, and rode slowly home in the dusk. Omar Pasha impressed me as being shrewd, decided, energetic, as well as an amusing companion, and a man capable of appreciating more of the refinements of life than I should have thought he would have found amongst the Turks; though he tells me he hopes, after the war is over, to be made Minister of War at Constantinople, and, – very probably, be bowstrung!

May 1st. – Captain Christie died this day at Kamiesh, where he was awaiting a court-martial, to consider his conduct with reference to the ships left outside Balaklava Harbour on the 14th November.

The decision of trying him by court martial, the worry and grief consequent upon so cruel an interpretation having been put upon the conduct of a man distinguished for gentleness, kindly feeling; and a desire to act rightly towards all parties, doubtless caused his illness and his death. Captain Christie was beloved and regretted by all over whom he had control. The masters of transports, I think eighty-three in number, had subscribed for the purpose of presenting him with a testimonial of their affectionate esteem.

I hear many of them have determined on going over to Kamiesh, to show a last mark of their respect for him by attending his funeral.

▲ Disembarkation of the Expedition to Kertch at Kamish Bournou, and the Blowing up of St. Paul's Battery', 1855.

May 3rd. – Expedition started to Kertch – 7,000 French, and about 2,600 English, with a few Cavalry; the object being to take and destroy Kertch, and to intercept the conveyance of provisions and stores into Sebastopol. We had ridden over to Kamiesh in the morning, and when we returned, we saw from over the hills the ships silently stretching out from Kamiesh and Kasatch to sea. We all hope much from this expedition.

May 6th. – The expedition to Kertch is returned, and, at the moment that I write, it is off Balaklava harbour. It was recalled by an express messenger. I suppose we shall hear more about this to-morrow, – at present, the simple fact is as much as we can digest. The sun is come to visit us once more in all his magnificence; and we should be able to give ourselves up to perfect enjoyment of the, to me, delicious warmth, were it not for the violent gusts of wind, which deprive us of all comfort and all satisfaction in our otherwise delightful Turkish tent, which is always, except when the wind blows hard, a charming place of refuge from the sun.
Yesterday, Henry and I rode into the plain as far as the Woronzow Road, – the extreme limit that prudence would allow. We let our horses graze for an hour on the thick, rich grass, which covers these most marvellously fertile valleys and plains, and then covered the dear old horse's head with branches of white May and dog roses, with a wreath of mignonette and larkspur. The mignonette grows in these plains in far finer specimens than are usually found in English gardens.

Monday, May 7th. – Stretched out again into the plain; this time, underneath the hill occupied by our Rifles. We crept up the green ravine between the Rifle hill and the hill in occupation of the enemy.
But the Rifles were amusing themselves with target-practice far over our heads; and the whistle of the balls, as they flew over us, made us remember that we were very much in the position of a brace of partridges on the 1st of September; so we turned, and reached home just in time to change horses, and canter over to the Guards' encampment, where we dined with Lord Adolphus Vane.

Tuesday, Wednesday and Thursday - Three days of incessant rain. Oh, how miserable everybody was! the ground ankle-deep in swamp, – a slippery, sticky sort of wet clay, which sends you sliding as though you walked on ice; while, at every step, it closes over your horse's fetlock-joint. Added to this, towards nightfall came occasional gleams of rheumatism glancing through the bones. I feel myself like St. Simeon of the Pillar, as Tennyson describes him, – *"While I spake then A pang of shrewdest pain ran shrivelling thro' me."* And all this cold, damp, rain; wind, and sleet have come to make memorable this tenth day of May, 1855.

Saturday, 12th. – Rode up the hill to see how the 10th and 12th had prospered during the wet weather.
Poor little brilliant Arab horses, they looked like rats that had been drawn through wet mud and hung up in the sun to dry. They were living cakes of mud; their long tails reminded us of ropes of sea sand.
Poor little gay creatures, all draggled and besmirched! Vicious to a degree beyond words are these fairy horses; and if they once get loose, they fly at, fasten on to, and tear each other with a tenacity and venom that I should have supposed only to have existed amongst women.

Saturday, 19th. – The first arrival of the Sardinian troops in Balaklava harbour.

Sunday, 20th. – Omar Pasha, who has returned from Eupatoria, whither he took flight the day after the one I have previously described, in consequence of a reported augmentation of the Russian force before that town, called on me this morning. He gave us a very pressing invitation to accompany him to Eupatoria, where he intends to go on Tuesday, and offered us accommodation on board the *"Valorous."*

Monday, 21st. – A match for 50l., between Colonel Poulett Somerset's chestnut, *"Goodboy,"* and General Barnard's brown horse, *"Coxcomb"* – *"Goodboy,"* ridden by Captain Townley, who had the reputation of being the best race-rider in India (he came over with the 10th Hussars, to which regiment he belongs), and who certainly rides like a professional jockey, and looks like a gentleman rider; and *"Coxcomb,"* ridden by Mr. Morgan, of the Rifle Brigade, son of Sir Charles Morgan, of Tredegar. *"Coxcomb"* was an easy winner – at least, so I was told; for the match I was not destined to see, as General Airey had very kindly lent me a very pretty horse of his own to ride; and which horse, never having been accustomed to a habit, fancied that by dint of galloping he could run away from it. This he found was a fallacy; but I could not bring him to the course until after the race had been run.

Tuesday, 22nd. – Leave refused to Henry to go to Eupatoria. 500 Cavalry horses went over from our camp to Kamiesh, to bring back convalescents, who had arrived there from Scutari. The Sardinians were disembarked in great numbers to-day; and, as we rode towards Kadikoi in the evening, we met two or three regiments marching up. Omar Pasha took a considerable Turkish force away with him to-day to Eupatoria; and those who were left behind, near Kadikoi, were changing their ground, and marching, with their frightful and discordant music, at the same time that the Sardinian troops were coming up the road. The dust, noise, confusion, and heat may be imagined, but I cannot describe it. The appearance of the Sardinian troops gives general satisfaction. The Rifle corps, which we met to-day, is most picturesque. They are dressed in a dark tunic and trowsers, with a broad-brimmed glazed hat, with a bugle stamped in gold on the front, and long massive plumes of black and green cock's hackle flowing over the left side of the hat, reaching to the shoulder. Their baggage transport is also well arranged. They are large covered carts, on two wheels, made entirely of wood, and painted light-blue, drawn by one, or sometimes two or three, magnificent mules.

Wednesday, 23rd. – A day entirely occupied with receiving morning visitors. Whilst we were at dinner, we heard some of the heaviest firing that we have listened to for months. Captain Lushington, who was with us, was at first anxious to go to his own battery, being alarmed lest the firing should be on the English, but after listening some time, we found that it came entirely from the French on the left.

Thursday, 24th. – The morning, till five o'clock, spent in the same busy idleness; but at five o'clock we ordered the horses, and rode down to our old grazing ground, near the Woronzow Road. As we were sauntering home, flower-laden, we met a second regiment of Sardinian Rides, and rode by the side of the regiment until we reached our camp. As soon as they came in sight of the Cavalry camp the men began to cheer them; and as they passed, regiment after regiment took it up, and such a storm of shouts filled the air as must have frightened the pale young crescent moon looking shyly down from the serene, calm, evening sky – such cheers as only Englishmen know how to give.

I have been much amused to-day by hearing of the theatre which the Zouaves have established at the front, and where they perform, greatly to their own satisfaction, *"Les Anglais pour rire."*

This morning brought us news. Twelve hundred French were killed and wounded, besides many officers. One company went in 100 men, and came back – 3. They had attempted to storm and take the Flagstaff Battery, and had failed. General Pelissier, who has succeeded to General Canrobert in the command of the French army, will doubtless fight it out again, as his chief characteristic seems to be most resolute determination, and disregard of all that interferes between him and his object. I think that General Canrobert's resignation of his post as commander-in-chief has given rise to many an expression of respect and kindly feeling, which would most necessarily have been withheld from him so long as he continued to hold a position for which it was obvious to himself and others that he was incompetent. This evening we made up a party, and rode to Karani, to hear the band of the Sardinian Guards. There was a crowd of Englishmen and Frenchmen already assembled. Perhaps it was because one fancies that every Italian must necessarily be a musician; but I certainly waited for the commencement of the music with an impatient interest with which no military band ever inspired me before. But to-day at least I was disappointed.

Beautifully they played, each instrument weaving its own peculiar harmony, with a truth and expression, such as could only be produced by genuine artists; but for to day they contented themselves by looking round at their audience, and – playing to them Valse and Polka, Galop and Quadrille. I fancied, as I watched the handsome swarthy faces of the band, that there was a proud look of concealed scorn as they regarded the waggling heads and beating hands of the admiring crowd. To me it seemed a derision, a mockery of music. We left early. While we were listening to the Sardinian music, the French were repairing their last night's work: they succeeded to-night in driving back the Russians, and there is nothing now between them and the town. To-day has been kept as the Queen's birthday, with a Cavalry review, at which Lord Raglan, General Pelissier, and Omar Pasha were present, with a very brilliant staff. Omar Pasha's dress was to my idea perfection. His dark-blue frock-coat, magnificently embroidered in gold, was fastened at the waist by a sword belt, the buckle of which, as well as the hilt of his sword, blazed with diamonds; a crimson ribbon across the shoulder bore the French order of Napoleon, while his crimson fez, instead of the usual tassel, was embroidered in front with diamonds and gold. The review was satisfactory enough. It was very hot, and rather dusty. The Staff in scarlet must have paid dearly in discomfort for the brilliancy they gave to the *"tout ensemble."* The 10th Hussars and 12th Lancers made a numerous, but I cannot think an imposing, show.

The remains of our Heavy Cavalry looked to my eyes far more soldierlike, more English, more solid. Declining an invitation from Omar Pasha to take luncheon in his tent, we rode straight to head quarters, where Henry saw, tried, and purchased a horse; and then we went to the plain below Kamara, where the Guards had games and footraces, and Lord Adolphus Vane an illumination in the evening, in honour of the day.

We remained until about eleven o'clock; and then, to quote the words of the famous Mr. Pepys, *"with great content, but much weariness, home to bed."*

Friday, 25th. – In our saddles by five, ready to accompany the Sardinian and Turkish armies, together with a strong force of French and some English Cavalry, who were to take Tchergoum, a village on the banks of the Tchernaya, and to establish themselves in the plain lately occupied by the Russians. The troops began to march at midnight; and consequently, when we reached the foot of Canrobert's Hill, we found the French Cavalry returning from Tchergoum, from which, after some sharp firing, the Russians had fled.

The French destroyed some of the houses, and plundered others, and then left the village. Seeing that it was useless to go to Tchergoum until later in the day, we followed some French Artillery until we came to a very handsome stone bridge over the Tchernaya. Here the Russians opened fire on us from a battery on the Inkermann heights; but though they fired several shots, it was at long range, and they did no damage.

One or two passed over our heads as we were watering our horses in the clear stream of the Tchernaya; and several more annoyed the French, who were destroying an earth-work from which the Russians had removed their guns. We ascended the hill, and had a good view of the valley and ruins of Inkermann; and soon after, finding the heat on the hillside becoming intolerable, we turned our horses, and proceeded, a party of five, along the winding banks of the Tchernaya. To us, who had not seen a river, and scarcely a tree, since our arrival in the Crimea, the shady windings of the Tchernaya appeared to possess greater beauty than, perhaps, actually belonged to them; though none but ourselves can know the wondrous luxury of riding through the

▲ The French Attack on the Malakoff 1855

tall and flowering grass, under the shade of oak and ash, creeping clematis, and climbing vine.
We crossed the ford, and let our horses graze, while we sat underneath a spreading tree. Some more adventurous members of the party found two fish-traps, full of fish, which we carefully put into a haversack, and then rode over the hill and along a lane, until we came to the height overlooking Tchergoum.
Here we found various parties of English officers, all exploring, like ourselves. We descended into the valley, but were presently warned that the Cossacks were behind us, and we must lose no time in getting away, which we did in as dignified a manner as we could. A few shots followed us, but not sufficiently near to excite any apprehension; and, clambering up a perpendicular hill, through thick masses of underwood, we got once more into our own country, and rode home in peace.

Saturday, May 26th. – This evening must always keep its place in my memory. We rode to hear the Sardinian band. Owing to a large number of their army having arrived, their audience was mostly composed of their own people. Then they played! Amongst other pieces selected for our enjoyment, was one with solos on the cornet-à-piston, which the maestro played himself. I listened with closed eyes, to shut out all this outer world of camps and trumpet-calls, round-shot, dust, and noise, that I might be alone with the clear voice now speaking to my heart. The music was so sad! it rose and fell like the sighs and aspirations of a soul shut out from Paradise, yet striving to enter in. Now there was an agony of wild, impassioned anguish; – now the notes fell soft, low, clear, and calm, as though angels had come to minister to the distracted soul.
Each tone spoke, – not to my ears, or to my heart, but to the innermost depths of my soul; – those depths that lie far down, as much out of human knowledge as the depths of the deep, deep sea!

Sunday, May 27th. – Rode this evening all over the valley of the Balaklava charge, – *"The valley of death,"* as Tennyson calls it; but it reminded me more of another expression of his, *"Oh, death in life!"* The ground lay gaudy with flowers, and warm and golden in the rays of the setting sun. It was literally covered with flowers; there was hardly any grass, – in places, none, – nothing but dwarf-roses, mignonette, larkspur, and forget-me-nots. Here and there we passed the carcass of a horse; – we saw five, with 8. H. on the hoof. Six-pound shot lay strewn about thickly enough, and pieces of shell. I did not see it, but was told that a skull had been found quite blanched and clean, with most wonderfully beautiful and regular teeth.

We saw to-day no traces of unburied human bodies, – the horses had all been lightly covered over, but many of them were half-exposed. We gathered handsful of flowers, and thought, – oh, how sadly! – of the flowers of English chivalry that had there been reaped and mown away! News came this morning of the expedition to Kertch. It was put into general orders, and read to the troops. Kertch was taken, without difficulty, the moment the allies appeared before it, as the Russians blew up their forts and retired. We also became possessed of sixty guns of large calibre, and many ships of transport, laden with grain and stores.

The Russian steam gun-boats attempted some resistance, but the *"Snake"* went at them in the most gallant manner, and very soon drove them back. General orders went on to say, that the Russians had sunk several steamships, and that our fleet is in possession of the Sea of Azov. The plunder, we hear, has been enormous.

No casualty up to this time had occurred in the allied force. We hear most distressing reports of the sickness among the Russians. Fifteen thousand are supposed to have been sent from Sebastopol to Kertch, Yenicali, &c. These, of course, are now (such as were not blown up with the forts at Kertch) distributed amongst the various villages, to be abandoned again as we advance.

Sunday, June 3rd. – Chiefly remarkable for a proposed ride to the Baidar Valley, which did not come off, and for a delightful diner à la belle étoile, which did. We sat on the summit of a rock, so perpendicular that one dreaded looking down its giddy height upon the quiet sea below.

At length the glimmering twilight died away, and, one by one, the stars came out. As far as nature was concerned in it, never was a fitter evening to conclude a Sabbath day.

Wednesday, June 6th. – I was extremely unwell; overpowered with the terrible heat, and weak and languid to a degree that compelled me, as I thought, to remain perfectly quiet and still. We intended to give our saddles a rest-day, when suddenly, at three o'clock, the guns pealed out from the front, and announced, with their tremendous voices, that the third bombardment had begun. We knew that this time the guns would not play an overture for another farce; so we ordered our horses, *"Bob"* and the pony, for I was unequal to riding any other horse than my *"sweet pony,"* and we galloped to the front. The first point of observation was opposite Sir George Cathcart's grave; our second at the quarries, further on. At neither of these places could we see the least what was doing, owing to the dense smoke which hung over town and battery.

Lady George Paget was sitting on the rock-work of the quarry, vainly endeavouring, as were many more, to trace the operations through the fog. We, who came up at so much cost to ourselves, were determined to see if possible, and rode along the front until we came to a post of observation opposite the Maison d'Eau. Here we saw very well, as the breeze had risen, and left the French attack clear from smoke.

Altogether, our observations to-day were very unsatisfactory, as the principal firing was on the Mamelon vert, which stands to the right of the Redan and Malakoff batteries.

We were told that the storming of the Mamelon vert would take place to-morrow; and as we were determined to see as much as possible of the working of the guns on that battery before the assault, we left the Maison d'Eau at seven o'clock, and, dining about eight, went to sleep earlier than usual.

Thursday, June 7th. – Rose at three. Started at four for the front, where we established ourselves in the piquet-house, exactly opposite the Mamelon vert. The firing at that time was tremendous.

Gun after gun, shell after shell, pitched into, on, or near the fated battery. Most of the embrasures were knocked in, nearly every gun dismounted. The Russians, who had already begun to fire very wild, only replied with two guns, one at each corner of the battery. These guns worked till the last.

Presently a shot came bobbing up the hill, like a hare, to where we stood, though we were not in the line of any of our batteries; but it seems that, whenever the Russians saw a group of people, they fired into them.

The heat, for we had watched (I confess to having fallen asleep in the middle – but then I was very tired and weak) from half-past four till ten o'clock, was getting intolerable, so we mounted and rode home by the Fourth Division. On our way home we met a French officer, who told us on no account to omit being at the front by four o'clock this afternoon.

By three o'clock we ordered fresh horses and started once more. As we approached the French lines of General Bosquet's division we saw the storming party forming up – five-and-twenty thousand French.

They stood a dense and silent mass, looking, in their dark blue coats, grim and sombre enough. Presently we heard the clatter of horses behind us, and General Bosquet and staff galloped up.

General Bosquet addressed them in companies; and as he finished each speech, he was responded to by cheers, shouts, and bursts of song.

The men had more the air and animation of a party invited to a marriage than of a party going to fight for life or death. To me how sad a sight it seemed! The divisions begin to move and to file down the narrow ravine, past the French battery, opposite the Mamelon. General Bosquet turns to me, his eyes full of tears – my own I cannot restrain, as he says, *"Madame, à Paris on a toujours l'Exposition, les bals, les fêtes; et – dans une heure et demie la moitié de ces braves seront morts!"* But let us ride up the hill to the piquet-house and watch from thence for the third rocket – the signal of assault. Our stay at the piquet-house is short, for shots are coming up there fast.

A navvy just below us has had his head taken off; and, besides, there is a place a little further back commanding a much better view. Here we can seat ourselves on the grass, and let our horses graze.

What a vehement fire! and all directed on the one spot. Two rockets in quick succession are gone up, and a moment after comes the third. Presently the slope of the Mamelon is covered with men, ascending separately and rapidly; not marching up in line, as our Infantry would have done, but scattered like a flock of sheep.

Two guns, hitherto masked, in the Mamelon open quickly upon them; but they rush up, and form when they reach the entrenchment. For a time we can see nothing but clouds of smoke.

The guns are all silent now, – nothing but the volley and file firing of musketry. The Russians, standing on the fort, fire down on the advancing French; but presently some men are seen leaving the Mamelon and rushing towards the Malakoff. They are Russians, and the Mamelon vert is now in possession of the French.

A momentary silence which succeeds enable us to distinguish musketry on our left. It is the English, who are attacking the quarries in front of the Redan; and an Artilleryman, who comes up soon after, informs us that the English have taken the quarries with but little loss, and, if let, will take the Redan.

But the noise in front commences again, and I see men in hundreds rushing from the Mamelon to the Malakoff. Per Dio! they are not satisfied with what they have gained, but are going to try for the Malakoff, with all its bristling guns. Under what a storm of fire they advance, supported by that impenetrable red line, which marks our own infantry! The fire from the Malakoff is tremendous – terrible: but all admit that the steadiness of the French under it is magnificent. On our left the sun is setting in all his glory, but looking lurid and angry through the smoky atmosphere, that is becoming dense and oppressive from perpetual firing.

Presently the twilight deepens, and the light of rocket, mortar, and shell falls over the beleaguered town.

We cannot hope to hear any accurate report of what has been done to-night; and as it is now ten o'clock, and too dark to see anything, we catch our horses and ride slowly away. Meantime cholera is come among us, and at Balaklava has asserted itself by stopping a career of much energy and usefulness.

Poor Admiral Boxer has fallen a victim to its remorseless gripe, and is buried at the head of the harbour, where he worked so hard, early and late, to endeavour to rescue Balaklava from the plague-stricken wretchedness in which he found it a few months before.

Friday, June 8th. – The French are in the Mamelon, where they found seven big guns, They have thrown up an 18 lb. battery, from which I saw them throw the first shot at the Malakoff. We should have taken the Malakoff but for a deep trench twenty feet wide and eighteen deep; and there was no reserve with trusses of hay to throw in, so the French could not cross it. We have nearly silenced the Malakoff guns with our fire to-day. They were burying in all directions. We lost thirty-three officers killed and wounded.

I have not heard of any one I know being killed. No words can do justice to the gallant conduct of the 49th Regiment; and all are full of admiration of the French, and the way they rushed at the forts.

A strong sortie is expected to-night.

Saturday, 9th. – Was again at the front, though the fire had considerably slackened, and there was nothing doing. But who could keep away from a place where so many interests were at stake? Not I.

Monday, 11th. – Took such a lovely, quiet ride to the Sardinian outposts, through a country of massive foliage, green hedges, and deep mountain gorges, to where a little village peeped out at us from beneath its heavy crown of verdure. The little village looked gay and smiling enough at a distance; nearer, it was all deserted and desolate. The houses had been plundered, and terribly knocked about.

I found a deer's foot, which I carried away as a memento of our pleasant ride, and which I shall have mounted as a riding-whip if I ever live to return.

Thursday, 14th. – The Kertch expedition has returned, and is in Balaklava Harbour. The destruction of Anapa appears to afford the principal topic of camp conversation. We hear that the *"Kertch heroes"* have brought home lots of plunder, and we are rather curious for their disembarkation. The success attendant on the expedition seems to have put everybody in good spirits; and *"We must have a try for Sebastopol now"* is the cry from the General to the newly-arrived Ensign.

I was occupied principally with a private grievance of my own, which, although to me a cause of very great annoyance and inconvenience, put me much in mind of the Old Lady in Albert Smith's ascent of Mont Blanc, who lost her favourite black box. This box (of mine) has been coming out to me ever since the latter end of February, and it is now the 14th of June! Disgusted by the delay which at first attended the delivery of goods viâ Hayter and Howell, this immortal box was sent out to me by what was to have been a shorter route; and after an expensive correspondence, an incalculable quantity of ill temper on my part, and a most vexatious delay, we heard this day that the ship in which this bête noire left England had arrived in Balaklava and had discharged her cargo. We sent down a man and pack horse to the agents of the ship, but received a message in reply denying all knowledge of the box. Next morning the same man and horse went down to Balaklava to the Parcels' Office. No box. Immediately on their return we sent them down a third time; this time desiring the servant to see the ship-master, and to go on board the *"Odin"* himself.

He did so, and returned with a note saying that, in consequence of a stupid mistake on the address of the box, it had been left at Scutari, where it had been delivered on the 7th of May!! It contains my summer clothing.

Friday, 15th. – Breakfasted with Général Feray, who commands the Light Brigade (Chasseurs d'Afrique), and afterwards rode, accompanied by his staff and an escort of Chasseurs, to the Château Periouski, a Russian hunting-box about a mile from Baidar. The ride was through a country absolutely lovely – a country of hills and valleys, green trees, and fountains bright, clear, and cold. The château is evidently only just completed. It consists of a large dining room, with a beautiful parquet, and several smaller rooms on the ground floor, and a turret and gallery. Except near the stables, where were two large rooms, there seemed no accommodation for servants. There was a granary, a coach-house, a four-stalled stable – such narrow stalls! – and a cow-house, carefully floored with boards, but looking clean and comfortable nevertheless. A garden all run to waste, and a perfect wilderness of trees, completed the inventory of the place. After we had thoroughly explored it, we returned to the camp of French Heavy Cavalry, at a village about two miles in the rear (Vernutka), where le Marquis de Forton, the General commanding the Heavy Brigade of French Cavalry, gave us a most hospitable invitation to a déjeûner à la fourchette, arranged under large spreading trees, the branches of which had been interlaced to form an arbour, and ornamented with masses of flowers.

In this delicious shade we remained chatting as gaily as if we had all been old friends, until the sun went down behind the cliffs on the sea shore, when Général Forton and some of his officers accompanied our party back to the tent of le Général Feray, which we did not leave until near midnight, after having passed one of the most agreeable days of our Crimean experience.

Saturday, 16th. – The Brigade of Guards marched up to the front, to be in readiness for the storming, taking, and destruction of Sebastopol, which is announced to come off on Monday next.

Sunday, 17th. – The guns opened fire in their usual rattling style, and had a magnificent burst of about half an hour without a check. They then slackened for a little while, but soon recovered speed, and went on at best pace till the afternoon, when they got very slack. But people seemed everywhere in the highest spirits about to-morrow. We remained at home till late in the evening, as several friends came down to see us, to say and to hear kind words, and to be wished good luck for to-morrow. About six o'clock Henry and I rode up to the front, not so much to see the fire as to shake hands with many who we knew were going in to-morrow morning. A few amongst these were, Captain Agar, Colonel Wyndham, Major Hamilton, Captain Hume, Lord Adolphus Vane. It was eleven o'clock before we reached home, and at that hour we found le Capitaine Léon Müel awaiting us in the tent. We sent our horses to have a double feed of corn.

I am sorry to say we have two horses out of four useless; *"Bob"* having hurt his heel, and the other, *"Chestnut,"* his back. Ordered some tea for ourselves, and then, having listened as long as my weariness would permit to an elaborate account of the wonders about to be performed by the French Cavalry and Chasseurs d'Afrique to-morrow, I crawled into the hut, and lay down for two hours without taking off my habit.

Monday, 18th. – At two, A.M., we were drinking some coffee, and at three o'clock we were at the front, seated on the ground as far forward as the Light Cavalry (who have been made into special constables!) would permit. We were a few minutes late for the opening fire, but in time for such a storm of shot, grape, shell, and musketry as had never before annoyed the ears of Heaven. We could see no troops.

The Malakoff is firing gun after gun, though as many as five of our shells burst in it at one moment.

The answering fire of the Malakoff is tremendous, and they have run up an enormous flag. The heavy guns of the Redan play away like so much file firing: the whole western horizon is dense with their smoke.

So long as these guns fire, it is evident these forts are in possession of the Russians. But the French sent down 25,000 men, and what with all our men told off for the storming party, such pertinacious resistance cannot last long; and if once we get in, the Russians will pay dearly for their obstinacy.

The firing, however, grows less: there are no guns from the Malakoff now. The great flag which they hoisted there is hauled down; and the Mamelon has been silent for some time. They fire a stray gun or two from the Redan; and we, who are looking on and wondering, inquire, *"What next?"* Alas! we are soon told.

The supports are seen moving. We fancy they are going down to the quarries to strengthen the force already there, for they disappear for moment in a ravine – but no, they are advancing towards us: they are coming away. The firing is over; ambulance mules are going down. So, then, we have been beaten back.

The Brigade of Guards and Highlanders who have been waiting on our right are forming in column, and marching back to camp. We too turn away – blind with watching, and stupefied with the intense heat of the sun. We meet countless wounded coming down. Sir John Campbell is dead, Colonel Yea dead, and Colonel Shadforth; while many that we know are cruelly wounded: there seems no end to the ghastly train.

Colonel Mundy, of the 33rd, shot through the thigh with a Minié rifle ball, walked into the mess hut of the 23rd, where we were sitting, as gaily as though he were untouched. Many soldiers, shot through arms and legs, walked up from the trenches, self-supported and alone; nor would any one have perceived their wounds but for the small hole in the coat or trousers.

How magnificent is such defiant courage!

Tuesday Evening. – We heard that poor Captain Agar is also dead! He was mortally wounded, and expired from exhaustion soon after he was carried back to camp. Poor Shiffner, who so nearly lost his life some time ago, is also killed.

Thursday, 21st. – The 10th Hussars are moved out into the plain with the Turkish and Sardinian force. The French talk of storming the Malakoff again in about twelve days; meantime, they are making regular approaches to it as to a town.

Friday, 22nd. – General Estcourt is taken ill with cholera. What a suppressed feeling of disgust and discontent runs through this army! It is no part of my business to enter on such a discussion, and I have hitherto carefully avoided doing so; but I cannot help sharing in the general interest and anticipation of a great and speedy change: men feel that their lives have been trifled with too long.

Saturday, 23rd. – General Estcourt is still alive, and the account to-day is more hopeful. We rode to the monastery, and returned in one of the most tremendous thunderstorms I ever remember The lightning was continuous and dazzlingly vivid, while the rain poured down in such torrents as to detach pieces of rock of half-a-ton weight from the cliff, and send them headlong into the road.

The waters too rose so rapidly that tents, saddles, and kits were all washed away; while near Balaklava eight Turks were this morning found drowned.

Sunday, 24th. – Poor General Estcourt died this morning. It strikes us that Death has taken the recall of those in authority into his own stern hands.

Thursday, June 28th. – We had heard that Lord Raglan was prevented by indisposition from attending General Estcourt's funeral, which was a strictly private one; and we heard yesterday that Lord Raglan's health was improving, and that nothing serious was apprehended.

Our consternation was great, when one of his staff, who was with us at the monastery, received a hasty message that Lord Raglan was rapidly becoming worse. I can hardly imagine a greater misfortune to the army than his death at such a moment as the present.

Now, when we may be about to lose them, we remember how valuable and necessary are his diplomatic powers in an army composed of so many nations.

We are almost tempted to lose sight of the inefficient General, in the recollection of the kind-hearted, gentlemanly man, who had so hard a task, which he fulfilled so well, of keeping together and in check the heads of so many armies.

Friday Morning, June 29th. – Lord Raglan died last night! It seems as though some pulse in this vast body had ceased to beat, the army is so quiet. Men speak in low voices words of regret.

The body is to be conveyed to England for burial. There is a report that Baraguay D'Hilliers is coming out with 40,000 men to land at Eupatoria, and invest the north side of Sebastopol.

A day or two ago, this might have caused some interest; now, for to-day at least, the thoughts of all meet in one darkened room, where lies he who a few hours ago was commander-in-chief.

Saturday, 30th. – The Russians, always aware of our movements almost before we are so ourselves, having heard of our loss, made an attack on our trenches last night, and were driven back with some loss on our side. I hear that thirteen of the Naval Brigade were killed, and sixteen of the Guards. General Scarlett and Colonel Lawrenson arrived in Balaklava yesterday; the former takes command of the Cavalry Division, and Colonel Lawrenson of the Light Brigade.

We are all glad to have General Scarlett in command of the Division, instead of the senior colonel, himself commanding a regiment, which is always objectionable, and indeed in the French service is not permitted.

I have been ill for some days, as, indeed, who has not? and would gladly avail myself of Captain King's kind offer of his cabins on board the *"Rodney,"* in Kamiesh Bay; but Henry dares not apply for leave, as the troops have no money. The officers' field allowances are all due to-day, and for the last ten days there has not been any money in the Commissariat chest!

The report in camp is that Commissary General Filder has signified his inability to provide forage for the number of horses now in the Crimea.

Sunday, July 1st. – As we were riding yesterday along the banks of the Tchernaya, we could not but remark the vast herds of cattle grazing by the stream, and we compared them with our own starved, over-driven, cruelly used beasts, with broken tails, and bleeding from hard knocks and blows.

The Transport Corps some days ago reported that they would not be in an efficient state until they had 22,000 baggage animals. At present they have between 8,000 and 9,000.

If Commissary General Filder's report is correct, the poor horses already here, and the hundreds that are coming out, may look forward to a cheerful winter!

The very idea of such another winter fills me with pain and dread.

July 2nd. – It is in orders this morning that the Cavalry Division moves out to the plain, in the direction of Baidar, on Wednesday next, to strengthen the position at the outposts held by the Sardinians, as two divisions of the Russian army have marched down within the last few days to the Crimea.

This will disarrange us all very much, we have become so settled in our old camp. As for me, when I look at the number of things with which I have become surrounded in hut and tent, I confess I can only sit down and shrug my shoulders, for it is absurd to think of packing in this tremendous heat.

Lord Raglan's body is, I understand, to be escorted by ten squadrons of cavalry to-morrow to Kamiesh, where it will be put on board the *"Caradoc,"* and so taken to England. Meanwhile General Simpson reigns in his stead.

▲ British Grenadier returned by the Crimea campaign in 1856 about.

▲ William H. Russell, Esqr., the Times special correspondent.

CHAPTER VI

THE FALL
OF
SEBASTOPOL

▲ Balaklava harbour in 1854

THE FALL OF SEBASTOPOL

"Giace l' alta Cartago, appena i segni
De l' alte sue ruine il lido serba.' – Tasso.
"Sebastopol est prise!" – Napoleon III.
Oct. 1. 1854.

LORD RAGLAN'S funeral procession from head quarters to Kasatch, where the body was embarked on board the *"Caradoc,"* to be conveyed to England, took place on Tuesday, the 3rd of July. It was escorted by several squadrons of English Cavalry, and the melancholy procession left head quarters after a salute of nineteen guns. Vast bodies of French troops, with Sardinian Cavalry, lined the road the whole length of the journey, whilst the mournful notes of the *"Dead March in Saul"* were taken up at intervals. I describe this from hearsay, as all those who were not actually engaged in the ceremony were confined to camp; in consequence of which order we were unable to witness a sight which I have since been told was *"too fine to be described;"* and also, that *"the Duke of Wellington's funeral was nothing in comparison."* From head quarters to Kasatch Bay is between seven and eight miles, and such a distance lined with the armies of three nations must in itself have been a magnificent sight.

July 6th. – Anniversary of my mother's death. For some days past I have been very far from well, and am now reduced to such a state of weakness that I am desired to procure change of air, if possible, and without delay. To this innumerable difficulties oppose themselves. There is the difficulty of Henry's obtaining leave, the difficulty of my getting over to Kamiesh, for I fear it will be many days before I can ride so far. I have written to Captain King, of the *"Rodney,"* to ask his permission to go on board for a week; but, with an ill-luck peculiarly mine, he is on the point of leaving that ship for the *"st. Jean D'Acre;"* and of course, in the confusion consequent on such a change, I should only be in the way. Meantime I must endure the mighty heat of this breathless valley as best I may, knowing that if I am to live, I shall do so in spite of everything; and if I am to die, so it has been ordered by One who cannot err. I cannot understand that inordinate fear of death, which possesses the souls of many. He who sees not as man seeth, and who can do no evil, will surely do with us what is best.

July 7th. – A draught of men and horses came out yesterday for the 5th Dragoon Guards. We had a great deal of thunder in the air, and one or two heavy showers, followed by bright hot sunshine. Several people, hearing that I was ill, kindly came to inquire for me to-day, as well as yesterday. How many friends has this break-up at head quarters caused us to lose! I shall feel, as I ride about the camp in future, almost as though I were in a land of strangers. Poor deserted head quarters! – the ravens always used to croak up there: they will croak twice as much now. The chestnut pony, sole survivor of the aide-de-camp's, came down to us yesterday, and, like another sleek and well-conditioned pony that he knows, he bears the name of *"Poulett Pasha."* – Poor pony! I think he had a presentiment that head quarters, and its comfortable stable and litter, was lost to him for ever – for he tried his utmost to conciliate us, his new masters, by licking our hands, and cramming his nose into all the pockets he could see, in search of bread.

July 10th. – The chances of my being able to get away, at any rate for some time, are getting less and less. Every body seems to be going home. I sent the first part of my journal to England by an officer going home sick; another, who has been out here about a fortnight, returns immediately from the same cause. Colonel Steele merely remains to wind up his affairs, and then he too sets sail for England. General Airey and Colonel Blane are alone left at head quarters of all my old friends. Mr. Calvert and Vico are there still, I believe. In fact, who would not get away if they could from the flaming sword of the pestilence? Omar Pasha has withdrawn himself and 20,000 men from Baidar, much to the dissatisfaction of the French, who reckoned on his remaining there until they had cut the magnificent grass of the valley and made it – oh,

English memories! – into fragrant hay.

Canrobert and 10,000 men have left the plain, and are gone up to the front before Sebastopol. From this it is augured that we shall, before long, have another try for the Malakoff. In Canrobert's division are included the Premier Zouaves, one of whom I overheard saying to a comrade, the other day, when they were both sitting fishing on the banks of the Tchernaya – *"Ah, mon enfant, mais, quand il n'y aura plus de Zouaves, l'armée Française sera finie!"* Thanks to the kindness of Mr. Vansittart, who lent me a very quiet pony, I was able this afternoon to leave the shadow of my tent, with which I was getting sorely discontented, and to reach once more the cliffs overlooking the sea. I know of hardly any more lovely spot than the one we chose as our resting-place this afternoon. Before us lay the sea, blue, serene, and quiet –

"Like beauty newly dead."

To our right and left rose the magnificent outlines of a coast naturally stern and terrible, but now bathed in a flood of rose-coloured light, with which the setting sun soothed the landscape, all flushed and scorched before from the power of his great heat; while round us, and underneath our feet, grass, leaves, and flowers looked up with pale, exhausted faces, thirsting for the evening dew.

July 11th. – Spent the morning in bewailing the hard fate which bereft us of our cook – a Maltese, who for some time had officiated in that capacity, having gone out one morning, and left us, as a legacy, the delightful intimation, that *"he was gone away, and warn't coming back any more!"* We soon fell in with a real Samaritan in Captain King, then commanding the *"Rodney,"* who lent us his own invaluable servant; but Captain King's subsequent removal to the *"St. Jean D'Acre"* obliged him to take his cook with him, and we are once more left servantless, helpless, and dinnerless. Feeling that we were doing no good by sitting at home, we ordered the horses, and rode to hear the Sardinian band. I had heard no sound of music for nearly two months, and when I pulled up in the crowd round the band I was in a state of mind that jarred with everything save annoyance, impatience, and disgust. ("Bob" had refused to jump a gutter, and eventually dropped his hind legs into it, though all the Sardinians were looking at him, – *"Bob,"* who is the best water jumper out of Ireland.) In fact, I was as much out of temper as out of health; but presently a voice, to which no one not utterly devoid of soul could listen unmoved, speaks to me in low and trembling tones.

Ah, where is the petty gall that *"wrung my withers"* not a moment ago? It is down below me, in the mire and mud of my daily life; while I am carried away far beyond this material world of trial and annoyance, and am walking side by side with angels – dreaming that I have caught the commencement of a harmony such as *"ear hath not heard, neither hath it entered into the heart of man to conceive."* Returned at half-past eight, or rather, I should say, fell crashing down from the top of Mount Olympus, where I had been conversing with the gods, into a soup tureen, and dish of fried fish more disgusting than anything ever produced in the annals of cookery.

July 12th. – I think I have a cook! We rode up first of all to General Bosquet, and afterwards to General Feray. We found him at dinner with le Colonel Polles, who commands a regiment of Zouaves, and who took pity on my distress. The French made a reconnaissance beyond Baidar yesterday – met a few Cossacks, and saw a body of regular troops in the distance. A large Russian force is supposed to be hovering about somewhere in the neighbourhood. Lord Ward's sale took place to-day, as he is returning to England immediately.

I was shocked to hear of the death, by cholera, of Mr. Calvert, who at head quarters filled the office of Chief of the Secret Intelligence Department. He had been consul at Kertch for some years, and was a man of great information, as well as a universal favourite with all who knew him. A few hours later we heard that Vico was also dead. How the plague festers at head quarters!

The perpetual presence of death is enough to make the strongest of us quail.

July 14th. – News reached the camp that a new Commander-in-chief is to be appointed in place of General Simpson. Vico's sale at the English head quarters. Tuesday,

July 19th. – A heavy cannonade was opened to-night by the Russians on the French left attack. General Luders is supposed to be in Sebastopol now; and we imagine that he ordered a sortie, as nearly at the same moment the Russians made an attempt on our quarries. But they could not bring their men on; and as we opened our heavy guns on them, they soon retreated, with loss. For some time after this they kept up a cannonade, apparently for the purpose of making a noise, as they fired very wild, and did not aim at any special point. They succeeded in disturbing everybody. We fancied that it was the opening of another fire. They kept it up from seven, P.M. on Tuesday, to about the same hour on Wednesday morning, and since then there has been hardly a gun fired by anybody.

July 20th. – Sat once more by the seashore in the quiet evening, saying over to myself the last words of Spenser's "Fairy Queen," at which the poet himself paused, and was silent evermore: – *"Then gin I thinke on that which Nature said, Of that same time when no more change shall be, But stedfast rest of all things, firmly stay'd Upon the Pillars of Eternity, That is contraire to mutability: For all that moveth doth in change delight; But thenceforth all shall rest eternally With him that is 'The God of Sabaoth' hight – Oh, Thou great Sabaoth God, grant me that Sabbath's sight!"*

July 22nd. – I have had to-day the pain of bidding adieu to nearly the last of my kind old friends in the Crimea. Captain Lushington, now Rear Admiral Sir Stephen Lushington, K.C.B., who was promoted a few days ago, returns to-morrow, laden with honours, to England. And well deserved honours they are, and must be, for this reason, that not one man out in the campaign has made a single observation implying that his distinctions were cheaply earned, or that he had been rewarded above his merit; and as such observations are very rife in the camp on like occasions, I think that their absence now is the surest sign that *"his honours do become him well."* I am writing late at night, amid a storm of heavy musketry.
Occasionally a huge gun flings forth its volume of death, shaking our hut and the table at which I write. All the Guards, and Sir Colin Campbell, are in the trenches to-night; Sir Colin going down as a volunteer, to give a little novelty and spirit to men who – God help them! – after being shot at every third night for ten months, like rabbits in a warren, require a little stimulus, not to give them courage, but to keep them from the heavy sleep induced by the overwhelming heat and the monotonous voices of the guns.
The heavy guns are silent now, but the musketry is pouring on, making ghastly *"music in the ear of night."*
I heard to-day of two atrocities committed in the army, and I think it strange we should have so few to record. One was a tragedy which took place two nights ago. Some Greeks – two men and two women – lived in a hut near the railroad, and also within a couple of hundred yards of a troop of artillery.
The people were honest and quiet enough, taking in washing, and earning money by various kinds of work. Two nights since, some Turkish soldiers went down to the hut, murdered the two men, after a vehement struggle, and clove the head of one of the women open to her throat; the other woman they stabbed in three places, and left for dead.
They then ransacked the house, and found 100l. in money – what enormous sums are made by the hangers-on of the camp! – and escaped. All next day the mutilated woman lay, the only living thing amid such ghastly death, and the day after it occurred to her neighbours to inquire why none of them had been seen on the previous day. The survivor is now in hospital, and has intimated that the murderers were Turkish soldiers, and that she could identify them. Only a week ago Henry and I took shelter under the eaves of that very house during a thunderstorm. The second story is shorter, and occurred some little time since.
A man attached in some way to the army, Commissariat or otherwise, was walking late from Balaklava to the front, having about him 120l. Some Greeks, who knew that he had money with him, had tracked and followed him until he reached a sequestered spot in the road, when they fell upon him.
He called out lustily, "Au secours! au secours!" Whereupon a French soldier of Artillery ran to his aid; but the Frenchman's eye detected the glitter of the coin, and, with a presence of mind truly admirable, he rapped the howling wretch over the head with the butt end of his carbine, seized the money-bag, and sped away before the astonished Greeks could at all recover their wits, either to cry out or to give chase.
So the Frenchman got the money, and escaped, while the Greeks were discovered standing, open mouthed, beside the corpse, and were carried off forthwith. Four squadrons of Light Cavalry – one of the 8th Hussars, one of the 11th Hussars, one of the 4th Light Dragoons, and one of the 19th Lancers – went out this morning to Baidar, ostensibly to collect forage, but really to keep the peace between the Frenchmen and the Turks.

▲ Captain Thomas Longworth Dames, of the RHA three-quarter length portrait, wearing uniform, standing near wall, bell tent in background.. Fenton's image

July 24th. – On the 12th of this month I was credulous enough to believe the asseverations of a French General, and a Colonel of Zouaves, who, with many protestations, promised me a cook.

I might as well, at any rate, have saved myself the trouble of believing them, for no cook, or servant of any description, has made his appearance, and the consequent discomfort of our lives must be felt to be appreciated. The cause of the heavy firing on the night of the 22nd was a smart attack made by the Russians on the French, and on our left attack. We hear the Russians were not repulsed until they had suffered severe loss. A messenger came over to me this evening from the squadrons at Baidar, telling me that they would start for a reconnaissance to-morrow morning, about fifteen miles further up the country. They kindly offered us the accommodation of a tent if we wished to ride up over-night and join them; but the letter found us smitten down beneath the fierce strokes of the mighty sun, far too weak and oppressed to think of undertaking so long and fatiguing a ride.

The report is that 300,000 Russians have just arrived in the Crimea; and as they are perfectly aware that they cannot be provisioned, they intend to seize on our stores, and drive us into the sea! This report is balanced by a fact that I happen to know – namely, that the Quartermaster-General has telegraphed for enormous supplies of wood, boards, and huts, to quarter us and our horses for the winter months.

July 30th. – A stronger will than my own, – one which the most resolute and powerful among us are obliged to obey, has kept me silent these few days. I have been ill: and to be ill in the Crimea is no light matter, as many beside me can testify. Poor Lord Killeen, too, is gone away to Therapia. In my distress I wrote to Captain Moorsom, of the Naval Brigade, to implore him to make arrangements so that I also might go on board ship. My position here is unfortunate. If my husband were ill – which God forbid! – he could obtain leave to go at once; whereas I am wholly dependent on the kindness of such as have not had all human feelings knocked out of their hearts. My appeal to the Naval Brigade was answered in a way that I must ever remember with gratitude. Captain Moorsom and Captain Keppel, who now commands the Naval Brigade, rode down to our camp, although the latter was quite unknown to us, and with the former we had but a very slight acquaintance; and in a few minutes they had arranged everything for my going either on board the *"Rodney"* or the *"St. Jean D'Acre,"* as soon as I am able to be moved. It seems as though I could never speak gratefully enough of the kind hospitality of these two sailors. Now, the only difficulty is, whether the soldiers will have humanity enough to permit Henry to accompany me. If they do not, I must go quite alone.

The dearth of any active proceedings at the front gives me time to remark on a little circumstance which rather edified me the other day, as I was riding home from an afternoon spent among the cliffs on the sea-shore.

At a little distance from us were riding three officers belonging to the English Cavalry, when we suddenly heard shouts and cries, and saw a Tartar running with all speed towards the three, holding up his hands, and apparently appealing for protection. The three rode on, until at last the Tartar, by dint of running, overtook them and tried to speak. With frantic gestures he endeavoured to induce them to listen, and with what success? Two endeavoured to ride over him, and I believe I am right in saying that one of the two struck him with his hunting-whip; at any rate, the arm was raised. As we rode homewards, I reflected on the vast superiority that exists in the civilised over the uncivilised part of the world: the latter, true to the old world instincts implanted by nature, appeals from the weak to the strong for protection – from ignorance to education and Christianity; civilisation (perhaps because he has not been introduced) rides over the man who is defenceless and wronged, or rids himself of him with the thong of his hunting-whip. Let us sing *"Te Deum"* for civilisation, Christianity, and the Golden Rule.

July 31st. – Heavy mortar practice all last night, with what result I have not heard. My husband has succeeded in obtaining leave to accompany me to Kasatch, on condition that he returns twice a-week to camp.

This permission is kindly given him by Colonel Shewell, Acting Brigadier in the absence on leave of Lord George Paget, and confirmed by General Scarlett.

Monday, August 6th – We have now been since Thursday on board the *"Rodney,"* in Kasatch Bay. The first evening that we arrived, Captain Charles Hillyar came on board, but only to say "good-bye," as he left the next morning in the *"Gladiator"* for Corfu, where he was sent to fetch up troops and guns. It is reported here that General Simpson intends opening fire this autumn, and with 400 fresh mortars!

Ah! what a sound will rise, how wild and dreary, When the death-angel touches these swift keys! What loud lament and dismal miserere Will mingle with their awful symphonies! *"I hear even now the infinite fierce chorus, The cries of agony, the endless groan, Which thro' the ages that have gone before us, In lost reverberations, reach our own."* The tumult of each sack'd and burning village; The shout that every prayer for mercy drowns; The soldier's revel in the midst of pillage; The wail of famine in beleaguer'd towns. *"The bursting shell, the gateway wrench'd asunder; The rattling musketry, the clashing blade, And ever and anon, in tones of thunder, The diapason of the cannonade."*

One would fancy Longfellow had been himself an actor in the weary tragedy that is dragging on around us, so faithful are his descriptive lines. During the cool evenings we sit in the stern walk of the ship, and watch the shells bursting over the *"beleaguered"* town. Last night there was a very extensive fire in Sebastopol, which shot its fitful gleams far up into the sky. The French must have made it doubly hazardous to extinguish, as they poured in rockets and shells as fast as possible, producing to us lookers-on a beautiful effect – a large sheet of light in the back-ground radiating on all sides with exploding fire-works.

The *"Terrible"* steamed away yesterday afternoon to Gibraltar for heavy guns and ammunition. We envied her the trip, for she will catch the cool sea breezes; while we, lying in harbour, surrounded by shipping, can with difficulty induce a single wandering zephyr to waft himself past our vessel.

Captain Drummond, who is appointed to the *"Albion,"* but is at present commanding the *"Tribune"* here, called on us during the afternoon of yesterday, and rowed us out as far as the *"St. Jean D'Acre"* and the *"Algiers."* Captain King, of the *"Acre,"* called on me the day before yesterday, and has promised to send me a piano-forte, which was taken from Kertch, and which is now on board the *"Princess Royal."*

I think there must be something in the profession of a sailor that makes him less selfish and more considerate for others than men of any other class. The Duke of Newcastle is on board the *"Royal Albert"* with the admiral, who has changed his position, and moved out, together with the *"Hannibal,"* the *"Queen,"* and one or two other ships, off Sebastopol. The Duke is reported to be suffering from the effects of the climate; and I have not heard anybody say they were sorry to hear it. If Cinderella's good fairy would but reappear and turn him into a private soldier in the trenches, in the depth of winter, I still do not think that many would be very sorry for him. Poor man! perhaps he was misled by false information after all.

A large American transport came in yesterday filled with French Infantry. The French have constructed a series of earth-works and redoubts, so as to fortify the harbours of Kamiesh and Kasatch, and also to take up a position (and a very strong one) on the rising ground inland, in case they should ever be driven back from their trenches. A French steamer, with heavy guns, went to-day round Strelitzka Point, and occupied herself for some five hours in firing mortars at the enemy, with what success we in the harbour were unable to determine; but at seven o'clock she returned to Kamiesh, bringing with her a smaller steamer in tow.

About four days since Captain Baillie, Lord Rokeby's aide-de-camp, came on board the *"Rodney,"* suffering extremely from an attack of one of our prevalent diseases.

Mr. Layard, brother to the member of Parliament (who, with a noble cause, and with half England at his back, contrived to ruin it), has died within the last two days, also on board a man-of-war.

I was interested to-day in listening to anecdotes of the trenches. Amongst them was the following: – The Guards have been engaged in trench work since the 17th of June, and have of course taken their fair share of the work. A few days ago Lord Rokeby was going the round of the hospitals of his division, to see that the men wanted for nothing, when he recognised among the recent admissions a young man who had distinguished himself for steadiness in the camp and gallantry in the trenches. On being asked what was the matter, the poor fellow said, *"I've lost a leg, my Lord. I and my two brothers came out with the old regiment: the first one died at the battle of the Alma; the second one had both his feet frozen off when we were up in the front, soon after Inkermann, and died in hospital; and now I've lost my leg. 'Tis not much to boast of, – six legs came out, and only one goes home again."* Profoundly touched, Lord Rokeby asked him whether they three were the only sons. *"Oh no, my Lord, we are seven brothers in all; but we three preferred soldiering, and enlisted at the same time."*

The *"Arrow"* gun-boat went away last night to Perekop, and the *"Harpy"* is under orders for the Sea of Azof to-night. Our hopes of a servant are small indeed. we have written to Constantinople, Malta, and England; and to-day I hear that General V—., the greatest gourmet of the French army, is at his wits' end to find a cook.

August 12th. – Went on shore yesterday afternoon, and inspected the dockyard, which is rapidly approaching its completion. It consists of several huts, two of them very lofty and very large; one occupied as a foundry, the other containing machinery of every description, worked by a steam engine in a building adjoining; machinery for turning wood, cutting and finishing iron, and performing all the work required for the ships. The energy and resources displayed, the use that was found for every bit of old wood or iron, the ingenuity which turned every material to account, made the inspection doubly interesting. Here were three forges, built of stone work brought from Kertch, of fire bricks taken from various of our own steam ships, a pair of bellows from somewhere on the coast of the Sea of Azof, and the anvils from the ships in harbour, or else supplied from England. A part of the machinery was of French manufacture, and taken from Kertch.

Saw-pits are being dug, pipes are laid down, bringing a constant supply of water from the sea, and the little row of store huts are each provided with a couple of buckets hung outside, and a large cask, half sunk in the earth, and filled with water, close to the door; so that there need not be the delay of a moment in case of fire breaking out. From the dockyard we went on to examine the stables and horses.

The stables are models of ingenuity and good workmanship. In some cases the walls are built of stone, with a wooden roof, the building divided into stalls, and the floor pitched with small stones, as neatly as we are accustomed to see our own stables in England. Where damaged hay or straw cannot be procured for litter, the stones are thickly covered with sand, so that the horse cannot injure the foot when stamping, as he does all day at countless hordes of flies. The Admiral's stud consists of six Arab and Turkish horses. One flea-bitten grey was a gift from Omar Pasha; but his favourite horse, and the one Sir Edmund usually rides, is a dark chestnut, very small, but well bred, active, and clean limbed. I recognised in one of the stalls a dun-coloured pony, which formed one of Lord Raglan's stud some months ago. We were shown, too, a wonderful proof of the efficacy of a little kindness and care in the case of a mule, which came to Balaklava in the baggage train of the Sardinian army, and having been terribly knocked about, and very severely hurt on board ship, during a rough passage, was left by them for dead on the sea shore. The boatswain of H. M. S. *"Rodney"* happened to pass where the wretched animal lay bleeding but still alive, and with the blessed instinct of humanity, he stopped to help the sufferer. He raised the dying head, and gave the parched throat some water, and by-and-bye he brought some food. In a day or two the mule was able to crawl, and, to make a long story short, when I saw him yesterday he was fat, and strong, and sleek; still covered with sores, which are in a fair way to heal, and following his friend, Mr. Collins, the boatswain, precisely like a dog. In and out into the huts, among the workmen, wherever his business on shore calls him, may be seen the boatswain and the attendant mule; and when he recovers from his scars, he will be one of the finest and handsomest mules that we have out here.

Such instances as these of kind-heartedness and humanity on the one hand, and gratitude on the other, are doubly pleasing in the midst of a life where we must, necessarily I suppose, see so much that is distressing and painful of suffering and indifference.

Monday, August 13th. – We dined last night on board the *"St. Jean D'Acre;"* and amongst the guests was Lord Rokeby, who is staying on board the *"Tribune,"* to be near his aide-de-camp, who is still in a critical state on board the *"Rodney."* Just before the party were thinking of dispersing, Captain Wellesley, also one of Lord Rokeby's *aides-de-camp*, came on board, and reported that the Russians were advancing on all sides, and that the whole of the allied army was turned out. The night, however, passed off quietly, and the enemy did not appear, and at daylight the forces were turned in once more. The reason assigned for the postponement of the attack by the Russians is, that a man of the 21st Fusiliers deserted early in the evening, and is supposed to have given such information to the Russians as would make them aware of our being in readiness for them at all points. I went this morning for a short cruise in the *"Danube,"* which, as tender to the flag ship, runs from Kasatch Bay to the *"Royal Albert"* some four or five times daily; and during the run homewards was extremely interested in conversing with an English officer, Captain Montague, of the Engineers, who has just returned from Russia, where he has been a prisoner since March. He appeared to speak very fairly of the Russians, mentioned gratefully the kindness he had received from Osten Sacken, and the hospitality which he had met with generally. Soon after he was taken, he travelled for more than a month in the wretched post *"Talega,"* going only eleven or twelve versts a day. He was detained for three days at Fort St. Nicholas, in Sebastopol, and one or two more in a house in the north side of the town. I was the more glad to have seen

Captain Montague, as he had spent some time with Mr. Clowes and Mr. Chadwick, both taken prisoners in the disastrous Light Cavalry charge, the former belonging to our own regiment, the latter to our brigade. He was able to give us favourable news of them.

Thursday, August 16th. – A grand fête-day with the French army and navy. All the ships of the united fleets were decorated, and at noon a tremendous salute was fired. About three o'clock, three of our smallest mortar-boats left their anchorage, and took up a position before the harbour of Sebastopol, for the purpose of shelling the camp and barracks on the north side, and the town behind Fort Alexander on the south side.

We went out in the *"Danube,"* and had an admirable view of the practice. The shells from the little mortar-vessels pitched with great precision, and must have caused no little consternation in the camp and barracks, as we saw many people running about in haste, and making for Fort Constantine. Presently a flag of truce was hoisted from the top of this fort. Our fire, however, continued, although it was principally directed on Fort Alexander. We remarked that, with a single exception, all the answering shots of the Russians fell short. There was nothing but feasting and gaiety on board the French ships. Sir Edmund Lyons and Sir Houston Stewart both dined on board the *"Montebello"* with Admiral Bruat, and before sunset the French flag ship fired a second salute. The medical inspector of the fleet pronounced sentence on me yesterday – namely, that I retrograde instead of improve as far as my health goes, and I am to go, if possible, for ten days to Therapia for further change of air. Of sixty shots fired by the mortar-boats yesterday afternoon, twenty pitched into the Quarantine Fort, but those fired at Fort Alexander were at too long a range, and all fell short.

News has this moment come in as I write, of an engagement on the banks of the Tchernaya. The Russians came down in force (I give merely the first reports as they have this instant reached me), and the French and Sardinians gave them a tremendous repulse, took their floating bridges, and drove them back, with a loss on the side of the Allies of 500 men. Up to this time I cannot hear that the English Cavalry were engaged.

Five o'clock. – Henry has just ridden over from Balaklava, and tells me that the Cavalry turned out at daybreak. The Russian army amounted to about 50,000; and they attacked the exceedingly strong position of the French Zouaves and Sardinians in a most gallant manner. The French, by whom the attack was quite unexpected, were very weak, as to numbers, on this point; the position itself being so strong.

The Sardinians, also, had to collect themselves after their outposts were driven in. The Russians crossed the river with determination and gallantry, and ascended the hill side of the French position. By this time French reinforcements had come down, and the Zouaves, leaving their camp, charged down-hill upon the enemy with their bayonets, repulsing them with fearful slaughter. They were also beaten back by the Sardinians on their left attack, materially assisted by our new heavy field battery (Captain Moubray's 32-pound howitzers), which ranged far beyond all others, and blew up nearly all the Russian ammunition waggons, dismounted their guns, and killed their artillery horses. The loss of the French and Sardinians was not heavy.

It was a brilliant day for our Allies. The English Cavalry was not under fire, except the 12th Lancers, who crossed the river, but were recalled immediately by Lieut.-General Morris, who observed that *"ces diables d'Anglais were never satisfied unless they were trying to get annihilated."* The Russians were all gaunt and hungry men, who had evidently been driven to death by forced marches. The enemy fired on the French while they were charitably engaged in removing the wounded Russians.

Sunday, August 19th. – Went to church on board *"The Royal Albert,"* by invitation from Sir Edmund Lyons. We remained to dine; and as it came on to blow so hard that it would have been difficult for us to reach the *"Rodney,"* we stayed in our most hospitable quarters all night. During the afternoon. Admiral Bruat came on board; and I had an opportunity of seeing, for the first time, the French Naval Commander-in-chief.

He struck me as being shrewd, and I was going to write false, but perhaps my meaning may hardly be understood; his manner was certainly polished enough. The two admirals sat in conversation, side by side, and the contrast struck me with such force, that I was obliged to lie awake at night to try and analyse it.

Monday, August 20th. – The sea going down slightly, enabled us to leave for the *"Rodney"* in the *"Danube"* at ten o'clock, after we had listened to the band playing on board the *"Royal Albert,"* and gathered a more

▲ Winter in Crimea. Huts and warm clothing for the army... by an artwork of William Simpson.

distinct acquaintance with the Russian works of defence than before. They are now busily employed in constructing a bridge across the harbour, so as to form a retreat from the Malakoff and Redan when we take triumphant possession of those two forts. The sunlight shone full on the face of the town, showing us long lines of windowless houses riddled with shot; and yet, standing in the centre of the town, one or two houses still intact; one a fine house, with a light green roof (I fancied it was only their sacred buildings that are green-roofed), and another house, solid, handsome, and large. Sir Richard Airey, who received an official notification of his promotion to the rank of Lieutenant-General, is also on board the Flagship, endeavouring to shake off an attack of fever which, like every disease in this country, however slight, leaves you weakened in a wonderful degree. There were two explosions in the Russian batteries this morning, but I fancy neither were of much importance.

Wednesday, August 22nd. – The *"Gladiator"* came up from Balaklava yesterday, where she had discharged the products of her trip to Corfu; she brought, in addition to eight mortars, 2200 shells and a couple of hundred artillerymen. I dined on board with Captain Hillyar, and there was a report that the French intended opening fire from their new work on the extreme left this afternoon, and that our little mortar boats were to go in, and throw mortars at the same time; but this did not take place. The mortar battery did not open, and although our pretty little boats got under weigh, they dropped anchor again almost as soon as they got outside. There was a telegraph made from the Flag-ship to Head Quarters about twelve o'clock, to the effect that *"large bodies of troops were assembled outside the loopholed wall;"* but they did nothing unusual this afternoon, although just before sunset a very heavy fire was opened all down the line of the right attack on the town. It was a lovely afternoon, and I walked along the shore towards the Lighthouse of Khersonnese. Here, driven almost on to the beach, I found the remains of a French or Austrian brig, which had been cast ashore. She was mostly broken up, and so close in that I could easily climb about among her rotting timbers. She had been laden with bullocks; their bones lay white and glistening all around; polished skulls, white as plaster of Paris casts, many with a bleached rope still wound about the horns, and several with the rusty shoe and large-headed nails adhering to the shrivelled hoof. I brought away a bone or two, more than usually polished, and a few parts of the fittings of the ship; and then, feeling that the sea was shaking the drift wood on which I stood, I carefully collected my relics, and scrambled to the shore.

Friday, 24th. – Went to stay on board the *"St. Jean D'Acre,"* anchored off Sebastopol, and remained on board some days. During my stay I had frequent opportunities of inspecting, through powerful glasses, the works, guns, and actual movements of the inhabitants. The bridge across the harbour, in front of the men-of-war moored at the entrance, which they commenced a week or two ago, is now complete.

The traffic over it is perpetual both of men and horses. For two days, the stream set principally from the south to the north, we fancied that the Russians were removing their goods, previous to evacuating the south side; and this appeared more probable, as they were busily employed in erecting fresh earthworks on the north side; but lately opinion has changed on the subject. It is universally believed that the Russians in the town are suffering cruelly from short rations and over-work. All deserters agree in the same sad story of sickness, privation, and distress. Meantime the town looks outwardly fair enough.

On Monday we heard that the Highland Division has been sent down to the Tchernaya, to strengthen the position of the Sardinians, as another attack is expected. The English Cavalry turns out every morning at four o'clock, and takes up a position in the plain, ready, in case of another attack from the hungry Russians. The reason of this daily turn out is obvious enough. There are only two outlets from Balaklava to the open plain, and a large force would necessarily be detained some time in filing through.

I could not but be struck on Tuesday evening, as I was watching the moon rise from the deck of the *"St. Jean D'Acre,"* by the wonderful and glorious difference between God's work and man's.

It was a picture composed by two artists. It might have been fitly called *"Peace and War."* Shining over the central forts of the town was the full moon, looking with calm and steadfast face out of the serene sky, in whose *"deep heaven of blue"* star after star trembled into life and light; whilst down upon the placid waters gleamed the pale broad pathway reflected from her beams. The distant hills wrapped in light haze were visible to the eye; but, immediately before us, no object save the grim corner of a fort could be discerned from the heavy, heavy weight of smoke that clung to and covered the city like a shroud.

Here and there across it shot the lurid glare of the guns, darting across the palpable atmosphere like a flying ball of fire. Who cannot see in this a representation of what has often filled his own mind? The wrathful stir of passion raging within, until calmed and softened by the blessed influence of the Holy Spirit of God.

Last night and this morning two explosions occurred. The one at half-past one A.M. I am sorry to say was in the Mamelon, where a shell blew up the magazine. This did, of course, immense damage; not so much to the battery, as to the soldiers. There were, I hear, above 200 killed and wounded. The explosion about nine A.M. was in the Russian works, but was not nearly so extensive. Lord Stratford de Redcliffe has been up here to invest the G.C.B.s and K.C.B.s. On his arrival and departure, he was saluted by the English and French ships. Being on board ship and away from the horses, I had no opportunity of going to witness the ceremony, which, I believe, was as imposing as uniforms, decorations, forms, and ceremonies, could make it. I cannot refrain from mentioning a brilliant little work entitled *"The Roving Englishman in Turkey,"* and from thanking the author for the pleasure he has afforded me in its perusal. It was put into my hands a short time ago, and since then it has sparkled on my table like a gem.

September 5th. – For the last three mornings in succession we have been kept on the qui vive, turning out the whole Cavalry at two A.M. and marching them down beneath the hill which hides the Traktir bridge, as, from information received from spies and deserters, the Russians have been meditating a second effort for the repossession of the Balaklava plains. They have been augmented by a large reinforcement of Imperial Guards and other soldiers, it is said, to the amount of 90,000 men. The attack, for which we have now been waiting patiently for three days, was to have been made by the whole of this force; 50,000 were to endeavour to take the Traktir bridge by storm, while the other 40,000 were to attack the French and Sardinians on the right and left. Rumours relative to the non-appearance of this army are rife. Some say that in marching down they met the wounded from the Tchernaya going to Bachsi-serai, and were so horrified at their number and their ghastly wounds, that they refused to advance, and more than 100 of these wretched soldiers were shot forthwith. Now, it appears that the whole force are either sent into Sebastopol, or dispersed on the plain of the Belbec, where they can get water. Meanwhile, we have opened a very heavy cannonade upon the town. The traffic over the bridge is incessant, and the Russians appear to be carrying all their valuables, goods, furniture, and pianofortes over to the north side, as we suppose previous to evacuating the south side entirely. Last night we dined with General Féray, and when we arrived we found him just returning from the front, where he had been inspecting the works of the Mamelon Vert and the Ouvrages Blancs.

During dinner, he told me that a Tartar deserter had come into General Bosquet's division during the day, and had told them of the agonies of thirst suffered by the army which fought at the Tchernaya on their march. Some little distance before they reached the Belbec, they passed some wells.

Order of march was at an end; the foremost threw themselves down headlong; the rest, struggling to get at the water, and impatient of those before them, drew their bayonets, and presently the wells were filled with upwards of 150 dead and dying bodies! I remember our own sufferings while marching, for short distances, in the hot weather in Turkey, and especially the frantic horses at Jeni-bazar, so that I can, in some slight degree, .understand the torments of the Russians. As we rode home from General Féray's our way was absolutely illumined by the light of a fire which seemed to set all heaven in a blaze. We could not see the fire itself for the hills which intervened; but, from the brilliancy of its light, we fancied the whole of the south side must be in a blaze. Not that Sebastopol would ever burn; the houses are too detached, and built so much of stone, that they would never keep alight for any length of time. The cannonade was densely heavy, and the light of the guns radiated off from the brilliant centre of the vast fire, and seemed like perpetual lightning. The French are supposed to have opened their new battery, by which they are to reach the ships. I am now on the point of mounting, to ride up and ascertain for myself what the light of the fire meant.

Ten o'clock. – The blaze of last night was caused by the firing of a two-decker, one of the ships in the harbour. Captain Keppel, to whom I went for information, tells me he fancies it was set on fire by a French rocket. However that may be, she burned away famously; the outline of mast, spar, and rigging showing with terrible distinctness in the lurid light. We reached Cathcart's Hill this afternoon in time to see a perfect explosion of guns from the French line of attack. Every gun and mortar appeared to fire at once; those that did not go off at the precise moment following with the rapidity of file firing. It was, indeed, *"a noble salvo shot,"* and was loudly cheered by the English soldiers who were looking on. Presently we met the brigade of Guards marching down into the trenches. The whole brigade goes down now every third night.

We were fortunate enough to see General Markham just starting for a ride, as we passed his quarters.

His reputation as the most rising man in the army, and likely to succeed to General Simpson's command, made me very anxious to see him. General Markham was formerly colonel of the 32nd, to which regiment Henry belonged. He is slight and wiry, with long grey beard, and eyes which, though ambushed behind a frightful pair of spectacles, I could tell were piercing and keen beyond most others in this vast camp. Having an engagement at the moment, he was prevented saying more than a few courteous words, and left us, with a promise to call upon us at his earliest leisure. The fire from the French lines still continues fast and heavy.

September 8th. – We rode up to the front again yesterday afternoon, although the north-east wind was blowing a hurricane; and for half the distance I trotted with my hat in my lap, and my left hand gathering up my habit to prevent its acting like a mainsail, and blowing me completely off my balance. We passed General Bosquet's division, and struck out the shortest track to Cathcart's Hill. A party of Fusileer Guards were marching slowly towards us, and close behind them followed a chestnut horse I knew but too well. Poor Captain Buckley, who yesterday was so full of strength and life, is being borne to the resting-place of many brave hearts, and will sleep on Cathcart's Hill. I begin to grow superstitious. I fancy that every man to whom I speak just before any great danger, is sure to fall a victim to it. Last night, on his way to the trenches, I met Captain Buckley, and he stayed a few moments to talk to me. Within two hours after I saw the last of him, spurring his pony round a corner of the ravine to overtake his men, he was lying on his face, shot through the heart!

I cannot watch that sad procession. I cannot picture to myself the frame so full of life and vigour yesterday, now a mouldering heap of dust. I show him what respect I can, although a black habit, and handkerchief, and a strip of crape round my arm, is all. He said he would *"live and die a soldier,"* and right well he kept his word. But I must turn away from the melancholy funeral on my right, and look forward at the siege.

There is a huge blaze in the centre of the harbour, and Colonel Norcott, of the Rifles, tells me it is a frigate set on fire by French shells. How bravely it burns! bright and clear as a wood fire in the vast home-grates at Christmas time. Presently General Markham rides up, and says, *"Mrs. Duberly, we shall have a fight to-morrow. You must be up here on Cathcart's Hill by twelve o'clock."* And then we ride briskly home, for the evenings are chilly, and the horses' coats begin to stare. As we lay our horses into their long, striding gallop, we talk of the prospects of to-morrow, and the chances of our friends – how much their number is reduced! Of Major Daubeny; of the boy Deane, who only joined last week, and will make his first entry into the trenches to-morrow; of Mr. Glynn, who exchanged only a day or two ago from the 8th Hussars to the Rifle Brigade; of Colonel Handcock, whose wife is with him at the front; of Lord Adolphus Vane; of General Markham, and many others.

September 9th. – Last night I was overcome with the shock of poor Buckley's death, and felt so unhinged that I did not start for the front until eleven this morning. The cannonade was terrific, exceeding anything that had previously occurred during the siege. After some difficulty in *"dodging"* the sentries, which General Simpson, with his most unpopular and unnecessary policy, insists on placing everywhere, we reached the Fourth Division just as the Guards were marching down to their places in reserve.

The Highlanders were the first reserve, and then the Guards. Here, I am glad to say, we overtook Lord A. Vane, and he promised to come down to us the first moment that he could get away, after the fight was over. I remembered poor Captain Agar's like promise, and my heart grew still as I listened; but we were advancing on the batteries, so we turned our horses' heads across the ravine, and rode up to the front of Cathcart's Hill, where we found the Cavalry at their usual ungracious work of special constables, to prevent amateurs from getting within shot. Now, in the first place, amateurs have no business within range; and in the next place, their heads are their own; and if they like to get them shot off, it is clearly nobody's business but theirs. The cold of to-day has been intense. Two days ago I was riding in a linen habit; and to-day, with a flannel wrapper, a cloth habit body, and an extra jacket, I was chilled to my very bones.

If hospitable Mr. Russell, the Times correspondent, had not kindly sent me down to his hut, and told me where I should find the key of the tap of the sherry cask, I think I must have collapsed with cold.

Meanwhile in the front nothing was to be heard or seen but incessant firing and masses of smoke.

The perpetual roll of musketry and the heavy voices of the guns continued without intermission, and the anxious faces of all were strained towards the Malakoff and Redan. By-and-bye wounded soldiers come up from the trenches, but their stories differ, and we can place in them no faith. *"I was in the Redan when I was wounded,"* said the first, *"and our fellows are in there now."* *"We have been three times driven out of the Redan,"* said a second; so we found that we could depend on nothing that we heard, and must wait in faith and patience. We left at about half-past six o'clock, thoroughly tired, and chilled to our very hearts.

Since then, within the last half hour, I have heard that Colonel Handcock is dead; and that poor Deane, the young boy, just entering into life and hope, lies in the hospital of his regiment, laid out ready for burial.

As he was standing on the parapet of the Redan, waving his sword and urging his men to follow him, a bullet struck him in the eye, and taking an upward direction, passed through the brain. His fearless courage, although for the first time under fire, has been several times remarked. I fear this is but too authentic, as our assistant-surgeon, who was working in the hospital of the 30th, assures me that he saw him brought in dead. The firing is just as continuous, – just as rapid, – just as heavy. I am told the Guards are not yet gone down. Oh! who can tell, save those who are on the spot, in whose ears the guns roar incessantly, what it is to see friends one hour in youth, and health, and strength, and the next hour to hear of them, not as ill, or dying, but as dead, – absolutely dead? Ah! these are things that make life terrible.

Colonel Norcott, of the Rifles, is a prisoner, and I hear unwounded. He sprang first into the Redan with his usual courage and recklessness; and the two men who followed immediately behind him were instantly shot, and he was taken prisoner before he had time to turn round to look for fresh supports.

He will soon be exchanged we hope. Meantime who will buy and keep that pretty, prancing, chestnut pony he was riding last night when he took his way with his battalion to the trenches?

▲ British light dragoons. Fenton's image

Wednesday, 12th. – Since writing the foregoing I have been three or four times to the front.

On Monday we endeavoured to ride as far as the Redan and Malakoff, but were stopped by the Cavalry, who were posted as sentries just this side of the twenty-one gun battery. On Sunday Henry rode up at eleven, A.M., and after making such inquiries after our friends as might tend to relieve our anxieties on their account, he went on to the Redan. He described it to me as a heap of ruins, with wonderfully constructed defences, and with bomb-proof niches and corners, where the Russian officers on duty in the battery lived, and where were found pictures, books, cards, and glass and china for dinner services.

Le Capitaine Müel called on me on Sunday, and told me the French loss was 17 general officers killed and wounded, and about 12,000 men. This I have since heard reduced, I think correctly, to 10,000. On Sunday evening as it grew dusk I ordered the pony *"Charley,"* and rode up to the Turkish heights. From thence I could see distinctly the south side in flames. I counted ten separate fires. It was a magnificent sight, and one which afforded me, in common I fancy with many more, greater satisfaction than pain. I could not think at such a moment of the destruction and desolation of war. I could only remember that the long-coveted prize was ours at last, and I felt no more compunction for town or for Russian than the hound whose lips are red with blood does for the fox which he has chased through a hard run. It was a lawful prize, purchased, God knows! dearly enough, and I felt glad that we had got it. On Monday I rode to see Major Daubeny, 62nd Regiment, Colonel Windham, and General Markham. Whilst calling on Colonel Windham, I heard of poor Colonel Eman's mortal wound. Our loss in officers has been heavy enough, I believe 149. In the 62nd Regiment 180 men went into attack, and 105 were killed or wounded. There can be no doubt that the assault was unexpected, and the Malakoff taken by surprise. The Malakoff was the key to the whole fortress; the Malakoff once taken and held by the French, the Redan became untenable by the Russians. We assaulted it after a curiously ill-managed fashion, and we were driven back. About that there exists no doubt. Nor should we ever have forced the Redan, unless the plan of attack had been entirely reorganised. Two hundred, a hundred and fifty, or three hundred men out of every regiment in the division formed the storming party. Men who had been fighting behind batteries and gabions for nearly a twelvemonth, could not be brought to march steadily under fire from which they could get no cover. As Colonel Windham said, in speaking of the assault, "The men, the moment they saw a gabion, ran to it as they would to their wives, and would not leave its shelter." Why not have taken all this into consideration, and ordered the newly-arrived regiments to lead the assault? – the 13th Light Infantry and the 56th.

By daybreak on Sunday morning, just as we were preparing to "go at" the Redan again, it was discovered to have been evacuated during the night. Malakoff gone – all was gone; and by night on Sunday all that remained in Sebastopol were burning houses, mines, and some wounded men, prisoners. The English until to-day have been denied admission to the town, except with a pass provided by Sir R. Airey. The French, on the contrary, have been plundering and destroying everything they saw. The town was mined, and these mines, going off perpetually, made it very unsafe for amateurs. Nothing, however, deters the French. Five officers were blown up to-day; and a Zouave came out driving a pig, carrying a dead sheep, a cloak, and a samovar, and wearing a helmet, like those which were taken at Alma, and brought on board the "Danube."

It is exceedingly difficult to gain admission into the Redan and the town. Until to-day orders were only procured through the quartermaster-general; but I see it is in general orders now, that any general officer can give a pass; and Colonel Windham, who commanded the storming party, and distinguished himself by his magnificent conduct, and his frantic efforts to rally and lead on the men, while standing himself inside the Redan, and on the parapet, is made governor of that quarter of the south side appropriated to the English. I need scarcely say, the English quarter is the worst, containing all the public buildings round the dock-yard, the custom-house, hospital, &c., but no dwelling-houses that are not reduced to the merest heap of ruins.

Thursday, September 13th. – A memorable day of my life, for on it I rode into the English batteries, into the Redan, the Malakoff, the Little Redan, and all over our quarter of Sebastopol. Such a day merits a detailed description. Eight consecutive hours spent in sightseeing under a blazing sun is no light and ladylike délassement at any time, but when the absorbing interest, the horrible associations and excitement of the whole, is added to the account, I cannot wonder at my fatigue of last night, or my headache of to-day. So many descriptions, pictorial and otherwise, have gone home of our own batteries, that I need not stop to describe them in their present half-dismantled state; so, clambering down (how wonderfully the Turkish ponies can climb!) the stony front of our advanced parallel, we canter across the open space, and ride at a gallop over the steep parapet of the salient angle of the Redan. "Look down," said Henry, "into the trench immediately beneath you; there, where it is partly filled up, our men are buried. I stood by Mr. Wright, on Sunday morning, when he read the funeral service over 700 at once."

What wonderful engineering! What ingenuity in the thick rope-work which is woven before the guns, leaving only a little hole through which the man laying the gun can take his aim, and which is thoroughly impervious to rifle shot! The Redan is a succession of little batteries, each containing two or three guns, with traverses behind each division; and hidden away under gabions, sand-bags, and earth, are little huts in which the officers and men used to live. Walking down amongst these (for we were obliged to dismount) we found that tradesmen had lived in some of them. Henry picked up a pair of lady's lasts the precise size of my own foot. Coats, caps, bayonets lay about, with black bread and broken guns. The centre, the open space between the Redan and the second line of defence, was completely ploughed by our thirteen-inch shells, fragments of which, together with round shot, quite paved the ground. We collected a few relics, such as I could stow away in my habit and saddle-pockets, and then rode down into the town.

Actually in Sebastopol! No longer looking at it through a glass, or even going down to it, but riding amongst its ruins and through its streets. We had fancied the town was almost uninjured – so calm, and white, and fair did it look from a distance; but the ruined walls, the riddled roofs, the green cupola of the church, split and splintered to ribands, told a very different tale. Here were wide streets leading past one or two large handsome detached houses built of stone; a little further on, standing in a handsome open space, are the barracks, with large windows, a fine stone façade of great length, several of the lower windows having carronades run out of them, pointing their grim muzzles towards our batteries. Whilst I am gazing at these, a sudden exclamation from Henry, and a violent shy from the pony, nearly start me from my saddle. It is two dead Russians lying, almost in a state of decomposition, at an angle of the building; while in the corner a man is sitting up, with his hands in his lap, and eyes open looking at us. We turn to see if he is only wounded, so life-like are his attitude and face; no, he has been dead for days.

A little further on we came to the harbour, and by the many mast-heads we count the number of ships. Here, too, are fragments of the bridge which I had watched the Russians building, and across which I had seen them so often pass and repass. There is a kind of terrace, with a strong wooden railing, overlooking the sea, and underneath us is a level grass-plat, going down with handsome stone steps to the water's edge. Following the wooden railing, we overlooked what had evidently been a foundery, and a workshop for the dockyard; Russian jackets, tools and wheelbarrows, were lying about, and hunting among the ruins was a solitary dog. But all this time we are trying to find our way to Brigadier General Windham's office near the custom house. To get there we must ride round to the head of the dry docks, as the bridges are either broken or unsafe. What is it that makes the air so pestilential at the head of the dry docks? Anything so putrid, so nauseating, so terrible, never assailed us before. There is nothing but three or four land transport carts, covered with tarpaulin, and waiting at the corner. For Heaven's sake, ride faster, for the stench is intolerable. We go on towards the custom house, still followed by this atmosphere: there must be decaying cattle and horses behind the houses; and yet they do not smell like this! Admiral Sir Edmund Lyons and Admiral Bruat are riding by, so we stop in a tolerably sweet place to congratulate each other on meeting in Sebastopol. We then continue our road to the custom house. What is it? It cannot surely be – oh, horror! – a heap, a piled-up heap of human bodies in every stage of putrid decomposition, flung out into the street, and being carted away for burial. As soon as we gained possession of the town, a hospital was discovered in the barracks, to which the attention of our men was first attracted by screams and crys. Entering, they found a large number of wounded and dying; but underneath a heap of dead men, who, as he lay on the floor, fell over him and died, was an English officer of the 90th Regiment, who being badly wounded, and taken prisoner, was put into this foul place, and left, as in the case of the hospital near the custom house, to perish at his leisure of hunger and pain. He had had no food for three days, and the fever of his wound, together with the ghastly horrors round him, had driven this poor Englishman to raving madness; and so he was found, yelling and naked. I think the impression made upon me by the sight of that foul heap of green and black, glazed and shrivelled flesh I never shall be able to throw entirely away. To think that each individual portion of that corruption was once perhaps the life and world of some loving woman's heart – that human living hands had touched, and living lips had pressed with clinging and tenderest affection, forms which in a week could become, oh, so loathsome, so putrescent!

At the moment, however, and I think it a wise ordinance, no sight such as war produces strikes deeply on the mind. We turned quickly back from this terrible sight, and soon after left the town. Riding up towards the Little Redan, we saw where the slaughter of the Russians had principally been. The ground was covered with patches and half-dried pools of blood, caps soaked in blood and brains, broken bayonets, and shot and shell; four or five dead horses, shot as they brought up ammunition for the last defence of the Malakoff. Here we met Colonel Norcott, of the Rifles, who had been reported a prisoner, riding the same chestnut pony which has had honourable mention before. Our congratulations on his escape, when we fancied him marching with the retreating Russians, were neither few nor insincere. The Malakoff lay just before us. I am told that it is, and it struck me as being, one of the most wonderful examples of engineering work possible. It is so constructed, that unless a shot fell precisely on the right spot, it could do no harm. What with gabions, sand-bags, traverses, counter-traverses, and various other means of defence, it seemed to me that a residence in the Malakoff was far safer and more desirable than a residence in the town. Buried underground were officers'

▲ Soldiers of the 8th hussar standing and sitting around cooking pots as a cook ladels food into a bowl; in the background stands a woman and on the left is the side of Fenton's photographic van..

huts, men's huts, and a place used as a sort of mess room, with glass lamps, and packs of cards. We are not allowed to carry any outward and visible signs of plunder, but I filled my habit pockets and saddle pockets with various small items, as reliques of these famous batteries and the famous town – lasts, buttons, and grape shot from the Redan; cards, a glass salt-cellar, an English fuzee, and the screw of a gun from the Malakoff; a broken bayonet from the Little Redan; and rifle bullets from the workshop in the town.

Then, as it was growing late, we rode back to camp by the Woronzow Road, and down the French heights on to the Balaklava plain. On these heights are still retained a few guns in position, which are, and have been ever since the 25th of October, worked by Turkish Artillery-men. They are famous for their Artillery practice; and when the heights were reinforced after the Balaklava charge, they were placed at these guns, with a French regiment close behind them in case they should run. With these Turks I have made quite a pleasant little speaking acquaintance, as we are constantly scrambling either up or down their heights. *"Bono Jeanna," "Bono atla," "Bono, bono,"* being generally the extent of our conversation, varied sometimes by *"Bono Cavallo,"* according to the province from which *"Johnny"* comes.

September 17th. – I went again last Saturday, provided with a permit from the French Head Quarters, to see that part of Sebastopol, and the French works which lie to the left – the French parallels running to almost within a stone's throw of the opposing battery, the *"Bastion du Mât"*, the Garden Battery, and the fortifications of the town itself. The French have by far the most extensive quarter, but I begin to doubt whether they have the best. We have such fine ranges of buildings for barracks; while they have streets of ruined dwelling houses, with the addition, however, of the Court of Justice, a very handsome building, and two churches. I was not much interested with what we saw in our expedition; indeed, we could not well be, for we were scarcely permitted to enter any of the houses without producing our pass, and making more fuss and chatter than it was worth. Many French and English soldiers had evidently been drinking *"success to the war,"* for they lay about in all directions hopelessly drunk. One French sous-officier professed himself so astonished and delighted at seeing an English lady in Sebastopol, that he induced us to turn back half a street's length, in order to present me with some *"loot."* I fancied, of course, it was something that I could carry in my saddle-pockets; fancy, then, our dismay, when he approached with the solid leg of a large worktable, with a handsome claw, about three feet high, and proportionably heavy. He tried to fasten it to my saddle, but "Bob" would none of it, and snorted and backed. We all, with many protestations of gratitude, declined the leg, and accepted a piece of Russian black bread instead, – more portable and more valuable.

We heard last night that the Artillery are under orders to be inspected to-morrow morning; and we also hear a rumour that all the Cavalry are to march up towards Simpheropol. It has been much commented on, that no movement was made by the army immediately on the evacuation of the town; and, on discussing the matter with one of the authorities, I was told that at one time we were under orders for Eupatoria, but next day they were countermanded. The Cavalry have done nothing since the 25th of October. We are now nearly 4000 strong, with an enormous amount of Artillery. Our horses are in good condition, our men very fairly healthy; and if they do not keep us out too long, and the Commissariat can be urged into acquitting itself with anything like decency for once, we may have a very brilliant little campaign of about three weeks in comparative comfort. At the end of three weeks the weather will become such that we must pack up, and be off to winter quarters. These are to be upon the Bosphorus. Oh! how we had hoped they would have been in sunny Egypt instead of on the shores of the draughty, miry Bosphorus, with its *"Devil's Currents"* both of sea and wind!

The Naval Brigade, now that there is no longer need for the Sailors' Battery, are all ordered on board their respective ships. I think there are very few but are sorry to leave their comparatively free life on shore for the imprisonment and strict discipline of a man-of-war. They would be (if we were to remain the winter) a very serious loss to us, as there were no workmen, carpenters, joiners, builders, half so handy or so willing to assist as those in the Naval Brigade. There certainly was no camp in which more kind consideration for others, more real active help, has been afforded to all than in that of the sailors; and their cheerfulness and willingness to labour encouraged and comforted all through the difficulties and sufferings of last winter.

I rode down to Balaklava a day or two since; and while the memory of the miseries of that terrible time are fresh in my mind, I may as well say how much, in common with everything else, Balaklava has changed.

It is no longer a heap of dirty lazar houses, infested with vermin, and reeking with every kind of filth.

Its principal street is no longer crowded with ragged, starving soldiers, hauling along dying horses by the head, and making the houses echo back their curses and blows until one's very heart grew cold.

Balaklava was then filthy, naked, and starved. Balaklava is now washed, and dressed, and fed. Balaklava was ugly and loathsome to see; Balaklava now is fresh, healthy, and even pretty. Neat rows of store huts have replaced the wretched houses of the Russians. The navvies have their stable at the entrance, and in the midst of the town is an open space; walls are pulled down, the road is raised, and a strong railing runs along its outer side; rows of trees are planted, and down the centre street the railway runs, giving dignity and importance to the place. Admiral Boxer did wonders towards facilitating the arrangements for embarkation and disembarkation, by the construction of his admirable quays, as well as by reclaiming the shallow water and marshy ground at the head of the harbour, which was generally covered last winter with the half-imbedded carcases of bullocks, and was always emitting a malaria most foul and deleterious.

I think the thanks of the army, or a handsome national testimonial, ought to be presented to Mr. Russell, the eloquent and truthful correspondent of the Times, as being the mainspring of all this happy change.

That it was effected through the agency of the Press there can be no doubt; and the principal informant of the Press was *"Our own Correspondent,"* whose letters produced the leaders in the Times, the perusal of which, in many a sodden and snow-covered tent, cheered the hearts that were well nigh failing, and gave animation, hope, and courage to all. More than once, when I have been fireless and shivering, the arrival of the then often delayed mail would bring me a copy of the Times; and its hot indignation, its hearty sympathy, and the mutterings of its wrathful anger have warmed me, and revived me, and made me feel for the moment almost like my former self. We are still in a state of uncertainty whether we move or not.

September 18th. – Nearly opposite the loopholed walls of Sebastopol, and about half a mile distant from it, lies a ravine with a church and graveyard, behind the French advanced works, and within easy range of the Russian shot. The tall spire of the church is covered, in common with all their sacred buildings that I have seen, with lead painted green; and it is only when you are close to the church that you discern the ravages of shot and shell. We turned our horses' heads down the precipitous side of the hill, and tied them to the churchyard gate. Trees of various growths filled the enclosure, and flowering shrubs, laburnums, and acacias, with clumps of lilac. Struck by the shots of their own people, the monuments and gravestones lay scattered and broken all around, while the sun, glancing through the thick green leaves, played upon broken pillar and shattered cross. How I lingered under the shadow of the trees! How the repose of the place and scene diffused itself over my heart, which never felt so travel-stained with the dusty road of life as now!

My life seemed to stand still, and be wrapped for the moment in a repose as deep as that of the slumberers around me, whom shot or shell could not waken, nor bugle-call arouse. At last I heard myself repeating those exquisite lines by some author whose name I cannot remember –

"Give me the soft green turf, the fresh wild flowers, A quiet grave in some lone churchyard's shade, With the free winds to breathe a requiem, where, Imploring rest, the restless heart is laid."

"Why Mrs. Duberly, you are a living representation of Hervey's 'Meditations amongst the Tombs!' For heaven's sake come away from the churchyard, or you will not be amusing any more all day." So I mounted, and we speedily got into the hard clattering road again, Returning home from this long ride, we were sensible of a sudden and keen change in the atmosphere of this always variable climate. The wind veered to the north, a cold deep purple haze covered the distant hills, clouds from the sea came up full of promise, not of a good hard soaking rain, but of that penetrating cold mist than which nothing is so chilling and depressing.

We lost no time in hurrying through the gathering darkness, back to the camp; and, having arrived there, lighted our stove for the first time this autumn. How comfortable and pleasant the hut looked in the warm fire-light! Thanks to the kindness of many contributors, I have been supplied with sufficient copies of the Illustrated London News to paper the walls entirely. This has afforded employment to my ingenuity.

But the walls when covered looked too black and white for my fastidious ideas; they wanted warmth, colour, and effect. I delight in colours. They give me almost as much pleasure as music. I like gorgeous music and gorgeous colour. I would have all my surroundings formed for the gratification of this taste if I could.

I have therefore tried to colour those pictures which appeared most to require it, and the effect on the walls of our hut is now, I flatter myself, good; at any rate they look home-like and soigné, which is a great point.

We both confess to an incipient affection for this little wooden room, where we have lived so many months; and we shall be quite sorry to leave it, never to see it any more, when we go down to the Bosphorus for our winter quarters in November. The facility of attaching oneself is a great misfortune. If it adds a little to the enjoyment of life at times, it increases the pain of it, I think, in a double proportion. My anxieties, for instance, when my dear friend and companion the chestnut horse embarks for the Bosphorus, will be positively painful to myself, and very probably a nuisance to my husband.

September 23rd. – After some days of cold and wet, mud and discomfort, the sun blazed out again in all his strength. Nature, washed and refreshed, looked red, green, and golden, in the warm autumn tints.

We came out like the lizards; and although there were still heavy thunder-clouds about, we disregarded them, and at three o'clock on the 20th started to join a party of twelve who were to meet at Kamiesh, and dine at the *"Luxembourg."* We were unpunctual, and started late; but made up for it on the road, or rather along the track of the ravine from Karani to Kamiesh. It was well we lost no time, as a thunder-shower came pouring down just as we reached the shelter of the stables. The dinner really deserves a place amongst the annals of the war, and is worthy of description by an abler pen than mine. But I most enjoyed the exciting ride home by moonlight, galloping along the narrow track, by furze and bush, past carcases of French bullocks left unburied, and lying ghastly in the moonlight, a terror to all ponies, and a horror to our own noses.

Every now and then a clink underneath an iron shoe tells of fragments of a broken bottle, but it is too dark to see; and a Turkish pony never stumbles or puts his foot down in a wrong place by any accident: and so on we go, our ponies leaning on the bit, till they reach the watering troughs of Karani, where they plunge their heads in to their eyes, and then walk steadily along the slippery slope of the hill side down into the hollow where the Cavalry is encamped.

The certainty that we are to leave the Crimea for winter quarters makes us anxious to revisit every part of its known world once more before we go; and yesterday we rode to the Sardinian observatory, a building erected on the summit of their highest hill, and from which a wonderful view is obtained of all the surrounding English, French, and Russian camps. We left this observatory behind us, passing to the right of it, and soon after came upon the tents which form the French depôt for General D'Allonville's Cavalry at Baidar. Beyond these again, on the extreme outpost, were Turkish Cavalry, and Turkish guns in position, overlooking a deep and precipitous hollow closed in with rocks. This was the neutral ground, across which Russian and Turks could glare at each other to their hearts' content. A dignified wave of the hand from the Turkish sentry warned us that we could not pass; so we rounded the base of the hill, and, by a judicious turn into a vineyard, came up with the *"avante poste,"* also Turkish, and were able to look down the dizzy height into the deep hollow. On every side the rocks rose perpendicular, stern, and bare, while far down beneath our feet lay the valley, clothed with trees and shrubs, appearing such a mass of verdure that the Tchernaya, which ran swiftly through it, foaming like a mountain torrent, looked but a silver thread wound in and out amongst the overhanging trees. A mill and a lane, scarcely perceptible through the trees, but running – the lane I mean, not the mill – close alongside the river, were all that occupied this profound valley. The only music to which that mill-wheel ever could have turned, – the only song the miller ever could have sung, – must have been the *"De profundis clamavi."*

The Turkish sentry close to us suddenly began to jabber away with a face of unmistakable delight. He had evidently discovered something, for his small, keen eyes were twinkling with excitement. The Turkish officer of the picket soon joined him, and, after some little conversation, turned to us, and said, pointing with his finger to the side of the opposite rock, *"Russes."* We could not find them, even with our glasses, though we saw Cossack horsemen further on. The *"Russes"* whom he saw were probably tending a large herd of cattle, which was grazing on the opposite hill-top, not 1000 yards from us. He took the glasses, and appeared much pleased with them. He then pointed out the Turkish Cavalry picket; and having remarked on the number of fires which blazed last night on all the Russian hills, we exchanged bows, and rode away; for the sun was set, and the moon looking at us over the shoulder of the hill. Nor could we stay to listen to the Sardinian band, which was playing on the plateau near Kamara, but had to make the best of our road to reach the camp.

Thunder-showers have not failed us these last three days. Yesterday morning the Highlanders at Kamara were deluged, and the watering places at Kadekoi were fetlock deep in mud – a faint foreshadowing of what the roads would have been after two or three months' rain, had not the siege been stopped, and all the army turned into road-makers. Beautiful roads are now being constructed: one runs by the side of the railroad from Kadekoi, joining that made by the French last year, and lately put in thorough repair by the Army Works' Corps; another runs from the Woronzow Road to the French position on the heights; while one railway is to be constructed from Balaklava to Kamara to bring provisions for the Sardinian army, and another to Kamiesh to transport food and forage for the French. The little stream which runs from Kadekoi into the sea at Balaklava, instead of being in a shallow bed, and deluging the plain after every two hours' rain, flows now between two high banks, so that it cannot easily overflow. It is really a pity – except, of course, on account of the trenches – that the siege is over; for if we remained here another year or two, we should be as comfortably established as if we were at home.

September 25th. – Yesterday, to everybody's infinite surprise and pleasure, Mr. Clowes, who was wounded and taken prisoner at Balaklava, walked up into camp in a shooting coat and wide-awake, looking precisely as if he had never been absent, and answering everyone's greetings with much the same sort of dignified composure that a very big dog exhibits in noticing a little one. I had taken an opportunity afforded by a flag of truce, to send him in a letter about a month ago; but he was then travelling down to Odessa, and did not receive it. He gives a most painful account of his adventures on the 25th of October, and afterwards in his march up the country. He was wounded in the back by a grape shot, which took him across both shoulders; but he rode on until his horse was shot, when he, of course, fell to the ground. Seeing our brigade returning from the charge, he tried to run after them, but soon fell down from loss of blood. His first thought was to lie quiet, and pretend to be dead, so that he might have a chance of escaping after dark; but he very soon saw parties of Cossacks coming down, who ran their lances into everyone of the English lying on the ground. Perceiving that the really dead were stabbed as well as those who pretended to be so, he rose, as well as his wound would allow, and throwing down his sword, gave himself up to a Russian officer of Lancers.

He took him and Mr. Chadwick, of the 17th Lancers, before the General, who asked them several questions, all of which they declined to answer. They were then sent to Simpheropol, and soon after they began their march to Perekop. They marched on foot in company with prisoners and convicts, and at night were locked up with them. They remonstrated, but were told that there were no horses or means of conveyance to be had, and that there was no other way of transporting them. Their sufferings during this severe march were very great; aggravated, of course, by the utter want of consideration shown them. The last part of the time during which Mr. Clowes was a prisoner appears to have passed pleasantly enough. He went into society, and travelled post. I think his case is a hard one, as he cannot get a month's leave to return to England, if only to provide himself with clothes. He has no uniforms, no kit, and has been obliged to buy back his own horse. Yesterday we rode up the heights till we overlooked Vernutka, and then returned by the good and even road made by Sir Colin Campbell along the summit of the heights, through his own camp down to Balaklava.

After all, Englishmen are not so helpless, so hopeless, and so foolish, as they tried hard last year to make themselves out to be. I think they rested so entirely on the prestige that attached itself to the name of a British soldier, that they thought the very stars would come out of their courses to sustain the lustre of their name. Alas! their name was very literally dragged through the mud, during the miry winter months.

Upon the strength of the evacuation of the south side of Sebastopol, the Fleet made a demonstration in their turn. They all got up their steam and their anchors, and sailed away, some to Balaklava, some towards Eupatoria. One of the first-rates crowded her forecastle with marines, dressed in their uniforms, and made as if for Eupatoria. This was merely a ruse, to persuade the Russians that she was transporting regular troops.

The Tchernaya outposts are still vigorously watched. The French have it that 125,000 men are encamped on the plateau and about the Belbec, with the intention of making a rush upon our position should we weaken it by sending any considerable force to harass the retreating garrison. The Russians in that case aim at burning Balaklava and Kamiesh; but their murderous designs do not prevent our sleeping just as soundly in the neighbourhood of Balaklava, or enjoying the triumphs of art in the shape of the *"Luxembourg"* dinners at Kamiesh. The Indian summer is come to us, and we are again almost complaining of heat at mid-day; whilst the clear sky and brilliant moonlight show us how enjoyable autumn would be in this climate, if we had all the advantages of the fertile soil, and could live in peace and plenty. The Russians, however, appear determined that we shall not have much peace. They have begun to throw shot and shell into the town from the earthworks on the north. One of these round shot came through the roof of Brigadier General Windham's house, and fortunately struck without doing any injury to the inmates.

Could not the fleet have so annoyed the Russians with their mortar boats as to prevent the construction of these works? – and if so, why did they not do so?

A French woman, riding in the French quarter of the town yesterday, is reported to have had her horse struck by a shell. For the truth of this I cannot vouch; but it is not improbable, as on the day I was last in the town, the firing was very heavy, and the riding consequently dangerous. It has also been said by General Morris that none of the French Cavalry will move into winter quarters, as the object of the large Russian force on the plateau, and by the Belbec, is to make a rush upon Balaklava, as soon as they find the army sufficiently weakened to admit of their doing so with a chance of success. We called to-day upon General Bosquet, who was very severely wounded at the assault on the Malakoff, and to our surprise and pleasure, he was sufficiently recovered to be able to admit us. We were shown into his room, which forms one of the compartments of a large wooden hut, and found him reclining in an arm-chair, having been able to sit up only within the last two days. He was struck by a piece of a 13-inch shell under the right arm and on the right side; it had completely smashed all the muscles and sinews, and his arm is as yet powerless above the elbow-joint. He showed us the piece of shell by which he was struck; it could not weigh less than four pounds. It is astonishing how he escaped with life, from a wound inflicted by so terrible an implement of war. He appeared cheerful enough, and glad to *"causer un peu;"* said he was ordered away for change of air, but did not wish to leave his post here, and fully coincided in my quotation, pointing to his wounded side, *"On ne marche pas à la gloire par le bonheur."* In his room was a fauteuil taken from Sebastopol, and which he had very appropriately covered with the green turbans worn by the Zouaves of his division.

September 27th. – News reached us to-day of two *"affaires de Cavalerie:"* one with General D'Allonville's division, at Eupatoria; the other with the 10th Hussars, at Kertch These reports require, of course, official confirmation; but, as the engagement at Eupatoria appears to receive credence from one or two French generals whom I have seen to-day, it must be tolerably authentic. We rode this afternoon to the Sardinian observatory, and, after admiring, as all must do, the neatness of fortification as well as its strength, we ascended to the telescope, which in placed at the summit of a high tour d'observation. By its aid we could discern huts in the course of erection, and the plateau by the Spur Battery, and could even see the Russians sending their horses down to water – one man riding and leading a horse. The Russian huts are wooden and like ours; while the Sardinians are digging out and covering with earth huts, that will not only be waterproof, but absolutely warm, from the solidity and closeness with which they are built. There never was such a pretty little army sent into the field as that of the Sardinians. Had they not established their reputation by repulsing the Russians on the 16th of August, they would be still considered in the light of the prettiest *"toy army"* that ever was sent to fight, each department is so pretty and so perfect – their Artillery, their Cavalry, their Guards, and, above all, their band.

To-day is my birthday, and in consideration of it, I was allowed to choose my own horse to ride, and my own country to ride over. I chose the celebrated *"Café au lait,"* that prince of pretty Indian horses, and rode him to the observatory, and back by the Sardinian band. Here we met several officers of the Highland Brigade, and heard that General Markham, on whom we had all built such magnificent hopes of British achievement under British generalship, was going on board ship ill; I am sorry to say, very ill, and it is said he must return to England. Coming out with all the prestige which surrounded his name, I think this sudden sinking into ill-health, and the abandonment of the army, will have its bad effect. We want good generals; we want men who are in a position to lead, not brigades, for we have good brigadiers enough, but divisions, or even the whole army; we want men with youth, energy, and courage to fight against and pull through any adverse fortune that may assail them. Our best general, our most unflinching leader, has been the Press. To the columns of the Times the army owes a *"National Debt;"* and so long as every incident of this war is laid before the public at home, so long as every man is familiarised, as it were, with the life of the soldier, so long will this war be a popular war, and so long will the sympathies of all England be enlisted on our side.

We suppose that the campaign for this year is over. The Cavalry, we understand, are to go into winter quarters on the Bosphorus. It is now becoming late in autumn, and the nights, and even days, are chilly enough. No orders have been issued, nothing official is known. Should it be at last decided that we really embark for the Bosphorus, I trust we may find ourselves transferred to proper accommodation for man and horse; but, if not moved before many days, to say nothing of weeks, are over, we shall be much worse off on the Bosphorus than we should have been, had we been allowed to remain on our old ground and permitted to prepare ourselves, from our own resources, for a second winter in the Crimea.

THE END

▲ A burial grave of the Sergeant Major Johnston, late of the 8th KRI Hussars, one of the last survivor ot the legendary Balaklava cavalry charge..

▲ British hussar in campaign dress during the Crimean war, 1855. By the author

APPENDIX, WHO'S WHO

WHO IS FANNY ?

Frances Isabella ("Fanny") Duberly (27 September 1829 – 19 November 1902) was an British Cavalry officer's wife, she kept a journal of her experiences in the Crimean War, including the Battle of Balaklava and the charge of the Light Brigade. It was published to great acclaim in 1856.

A second book followed a few years later, giving her account of the suppression of the Sepoy Mutiny (the Indian Rebellion of 1857). Her husband, Captain Henry Duberly, was paymaster to the 8th Royal Irish Hussars, part of the British light cavalry that took part in the Charge of the Light Brigade. Duberley's journal of her time in the Crimea was published as Journal Kept During the Russian War. It not only includes eye-witness accounts, but is also a record of gossip and rumours circulating in the British Army.

First years

Frances Isabella Locke was born in 1829, at Rowdeford House in the village of Rowde, near Devizes in Wiltshire. The youngest (of nine children) daughter of Wadham Locke, Duberly has been described as *"a splendid rider, witty, ambitious, daring, lively, loquacious and gregarious."* She seemed to possess the physical requirements and tough attitude required of her surroundings, saying that she *"was awoke by the reveille at half-past two; rose, packed our bedding and tent, got a stale egg and a mouthful of brandy, and was in my saddle by half-past five."*

After the death of her mother in 1838, she moved to live with her eldest brother (also Wadham Locke) at Ashton Gifford House in Wiltshire. She left Ashton Gifford on her marriage in 1845, which took place shortly after her brother had married for a second time.

Fanny and Henry in Crimea

Duberly travelled with her husband to the Crimea in 1854 and stayed with him throughout his time there, despite the protests of commanders such as Lord Lucan. As the only officer's wife at the front, she was a centre of attention. She was told of planned attacks ahead of time, giving her the opportunity to be in a good position to witness them. Such was the case at the Battle of Balaclava, where her journey from camp to meet up with Henry and watch the battle took her quite close to the enemy. Though her husband survived the day (being away on staff duties), many of her friends did not: *"Even my closed eyelids were filled with the ruddy glare of blood."* Being so close to the front line in one of the first "modern" wars, Mrs Duberly differed from many of her compatriots back home in comprehending the reality of war. When her husband asked if she wanted to view the aftermath of the Battle of Inkerman, she told him she could not as *"the thought of it made me shutter [sic] and turn sick."*.

Duberly's adventures did not always sit well with society. She was pointedly snubbed at the Royal review of her husband's regiment after the war. The journal she published after the war had originally been intended to have a dedication to Queen Victoria, but this was refused, much to her dismay. Nonetheless she was popular with the troops (who nicknamed her "Mrs. Jubilee") and many people in England. Her published journal met with some success and prints of a photo of her taken by Roger Fenton sold quite well. In this image we may see the Captain Henry Duberly standing before Isabella Duberly who is on horseback.

India

Duberly again accompanied her husband when the 8th Hussars were sent to India in 1856. She stayed with him throughout the final months of the Sepoy Mutiny. She was adamant about accompanying the troops on campaign and told her sister that she would *"stain my face and hands and adopt the Hindoo caftan and turban,"* refusing to stay behind. At Gwalior in 1858, while watching the start of a cavalry charge, her horse ran after the rest and, instead of holding back, she told her husband *"I must go!"* and galloped away.

▲ Captain Henry Duberly, paymaster of the 8th Hussars, with his wife Frances Isabella during the Crimean war, 1855.
Photograph: Roger Fenton.

► Roger Fenton selfportrait in 1852 about.

Married life

The Duberlys had no children. She was a great friend and supporter of her husband, who never seemed to be jealous of his wife as the centre of attention in the all-male environment of the British Army in the field. She described her husband as *"a friend I am obliged to support."* He was ill when the time came to go ashore in the Crimea and she told her sister that *"Lord Cardigan intends him to land with the troops, but I don't intend him to do so."* The Duberlys had their differences of opinion on the nature of military service. When orders came from Lucan that she must be put ashore at Constantinople, she wrote that "Henry looks upon the order as a soldier; I as a woman, and laugh at it.".

The Duberlys returned to England in 1864. She retained her campaign memories but, when asked to reminisce about what she had witnessed, she replied that *"those days are best forgotten."* Nevertheless, she retained her adventurous spirit and complained to a nephew in 1896 that *"I cannot stand dullness for long, and life gets duller and duller as one gets older."*.

She died at Cheltenham in 1902, aged 73.

WHO IS ROGER ?

Roger Fenton Roger Fenton was born in Crimble Hall, then within the parish of Bury, Lancashire, on 28 March 1819. His grandfather was a wealthy cotton manufacturer and banker, his father a banker and Member of Parliament. Roger was the fourth of seven children by his father's first marriage. His father had 10 more children by his second wife. Today everybody remembers the figure of Fenton as a pioneering British photographer, probably the first war photographers. Fenton is a towering figure in the history of photography, the most celebrated and influential photographer in England during the medium's "golden age" of the 1850s. Before taking up the camera, he studied law in London and painting in Paris. During a visit to the Great Exhibition in Hyde Park in London in 1851 Fenton was impressed by the photography on display there. He then visited Paris to learn the waxed paper calotype process, most likely from Gustave Le Gray who had modified the methods employed by William Henry Fox Talbot, its inventor. By 1852 He traveled and photographed the Russian landmarks of Kiev and Moscow; founded the Photographic Society (later designated the Royal Photographic Society) in 1853; was appointed the first official photographer of the British Museum in 1854; achieved widespread recognition for his photographs of the Crimean War in 1855; and excelled throughout the decade as a photographer in all the medium's genres—architecture, landscape, portraiture, still life, reportage, and tableau-vivant.

Crimean War

Fenton's most widespread acclaim came in 1855, with photographs of the Crimean War, a conflict in which British, French, Sardinian, and Turkish troops battled Russia's attempt to expand its influence into European territory of the Ottoman Empire. Fenton was commissioned by the Manchester publisher Thomas Agnew & Sons to travel to the Crimea and document the war, and his mission was encouraged by the government, which hoped that his photographs would reassure a worried public. Fenton's extensive documentation of the war—the first such use of photography—included pictures of the port of Balaklava, the camps, the terrain of battle, and portraits of officers, soldiers, and support staff of the various allied armies.

Post Crimea

Undaunted by the lack of commercial success for his Crimean photographs, Fenton remained driven with great energy to perfect his art and to record meaningful and artistic images. He travelled widely over Britain to record landscapes and still life images, but as time moved on, photography was becoming more accessible. Many, with sufficient knowledge and also the hunger to develop business, sought to profit from selling quick portraits to common people. It is likely that Fenton, from a wealthy background, disdained 'trade' photographers, but nevertheless still wanted to profit from the art by taking exclusive images and selling them at good prices. He thus fell into conflict with many of his peers who genuinely needed to make money from photography and were willing to 'cheapen their art' (as Fenton saw it), and also with the Photographic Society, who believed that no photographer should soil himself with the 'sin' of exploiting his talent commercially in any manner.

In 1862, after a final series of photographs—a remarkable group of lush still lifes—Fenton sold his equipment and negatives, resigned from the Royal Photographic Society, and returned to his new home a Potter' Bar, Hertfordshire where He died the 8 august 1869 after a week-long illness - he was only 50 yrs old. In the course of a single decade, Fenton had played a pivotal role—by advocacy and example—in demonstrating that photography could rival drawing and painting not only as a means of conveying information, but also as a medium of visual delight and powerful expression.

BIBLIOGRAPHY

Arnold, Guy. Historical dictionary of the Crimean War (Scarecrow Press, 2002)

Troubetzkoy, Alexis A Brief History of the Crimean War (Constable & Robinson, 2006),

Badem, Candan. The Ottoman Crimean War (1853–1856) (Leiden: Brill, 2010). 432 pp.

Bridge and Bullen, The Great Powers and the European States System 1814–1914, (Pearson Education: London), 2005

Bamgart, Winfried The Crimean War, 1853–1856 (2002) Arnold Publishers

Cox, Michael, and John Lenton. Crimean War Basics: Organisation and Uniforms: Russia and Turkey (1997)

Curtiss, John Shelton. Russia's Crimean War (1979)

Figes, Orlando. Crimea: The Last Crusade (2010) Allen Lane. the standard scholarly study; American edition published as The Crimean War: A History (2010)

Goldfrank, David M. The Origins of the Crimean War (1993)

Gorizontov, Leonid E (2012). "The Crimean War as a Test of Russia's Imperial Durability". Russian Studies in History 51 (1): 65–94.

Greenwood, Adrian (2015). Victoria's Scottish Lion: The Life of Colin Campbell, Lord Clyde. UK: History Press. p. 496.

Hoppen, K. Theodore. The Mid-Victorian Generation, 1846–1886 (1998) pp. 167–83; summary of British policy online

Lambert, Andrew (1989). "Preparing for the Russian War: British Strategic Planning, March, 1853 – March 1854".

Lambert, Andrew (2013). The Crimean War: British Grand Strategy against Russia, 1853–56. Ashgate Publishing. argues that the Baltic was the decisive theatre

Markovits, Stefanie. The Crimean War in the British Imagination (Cambridge University Press, 2010)

Pearce, Robert. "The Results of the Crimean War," History Review (2011) #70 pp. 27–33.

Ponting, Clive The Crimean War (2004) Chatto and Windus ISBN 0-7011-7390-4

Pottinger Saab, Anne The Origins of the Crimean Alliance (1977) University of Virginia Press

Puryear, Vernon J (1931). "New Light on the Origins of the Crimean War". Journal of Modern History 3

Ramm, Agatha, and B. H. Sumner. "The Crimean War." in J.P.T. Bury, ed., The New Cambridge Modern History: Volume 10: The Zenith of European Power, 1830–1870 (1960) pp. 468–92.

Rich, Norman Why the Crimean War: A Cautionary Tale (1985) McGraw-Hill

Ridley, Jasper. Lord Palmerston (1970) pp. 425–54

Royle, Trevor Crimea: The Great Crimean War, 1854–1856 (2000) Palgrave Macmillan

Schroeder, Paul W. Austria, Great Britain, and the Crimean War: The Destruction of the European Concert (Cornell Up, 192) online

Schmitt, Bernadotte E (1919). "The Diplomatic Preliminaries of the Crimean War". American Historical Review 25 (1): 36–67.

Small, Hugh. The Crimean War: Queen Victoria's War with the Russian Tsars (Tempus, 2007); diplomacy, pp. 62–82

Strachan, Hew (1978). "Soldiers, Strategy and Sebastopol". Historical Journal 21 (2): 303–325.

Taylor, A.J.P. The Struggle for Mastery in Europe: 1848–1918 (1954) pp. 62–82

Troubetzkoy, Alexis (2006). A Brief History of the Crimean War. London: Constable & Robinson.

Wetzel, David The Crimean War: A Diplomatic History (1985) Columbia University Press

Zayonchkovski, Andrei (2002) [1908–1913]. Восточная война 1853–1856 Eastern War 1853–1856. Великие противостояния. Petersburg

HISTORIOGRAPHY AND MEMORY

Gooch, Brison D. "A Century of Historiography on the Origins of the Crimean War", American Historical Review Vol. 62, No. 1 (Oct. 1956), pp. 33–58 in JSTOR

Edgerton, Robert B. Death or Glory: The Legacy of the Crimean War (1999) online

Kozelsky, Mara. "The Crimean War, 1853–56," Kritika (2012) 13#4 online

Lambert, Albert (2003). "Crimean War 1853–1856," in David Loades, ed.". Reader's Guide to British History 1: 318–19.

Lambert, Andrew. The Crimean War: British Grand Strategy Against Russia, 1853–56 (2nd ed. Ashgate, 2011) the 2nd edition has a detailed summary of the historiography, pp. 1–20

Markovits, Stefanie. The Crimean War in the British Imagination (Cambridge University Press: 2009) 287 pp.

Russell, William Howard, The Crimean War: As Seen by Those Who Reported It (Louisiana State University Press, 2009)

Small, Hugh. "Sebastopol Besieged," History Today (2014) 64#4 pp. 20–21

CONTEMPORARY SOURCES

John Miller Adye (1860). A Review of the Crimean War to the winter of 1854–5. Hurst and Blackett.

Alexander William Kinglake (1863–87). The Invasion of the Crimea, (nine volumes, London): vol1 – vol2 – vol3 – vol4 – vol5 – vol6 – vol7 – vol8 – vol9

William Howard Russell (1855). The War (volume 1): from the Landing at Gallipoli to the Death of Lord Raglan. George Routledge & Co.

William Howard Russell (1856). The War (volume 2): from the death of Lord Raglan to the evacuation of the Crimea. George Routledge & Co.

William Howard Russell (1877). The British expedition to the Crimea. G. Routledge and Sons.

Adolphus Slade (1867). Turkey and the Crimean War: a narrative of historical events. Smith, Elder & Co.

WITNESS TO HISTORY

Our new series of books of history, based on eyewitnesses, or the great storytellers and war correspondents of the great events of world history: battles, sieges, military campaigns, but also travels and discoveries. New books from old books, completely revised and illustrated by Soldiershop! Our edition, the first ever published in English, available both on paperback and digital format, richly illustrated with unpublished and colored plates.
Available also in ebook!

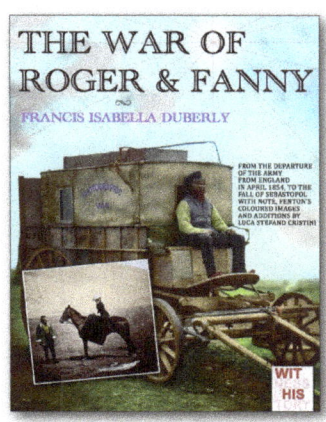

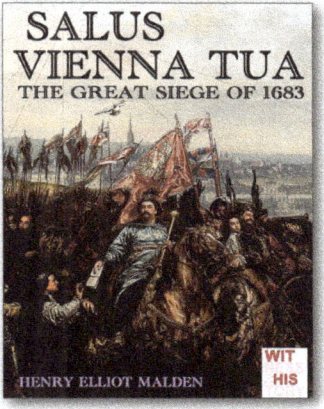

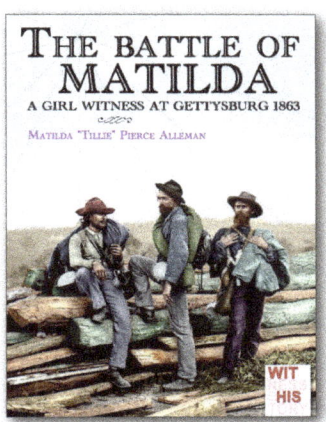

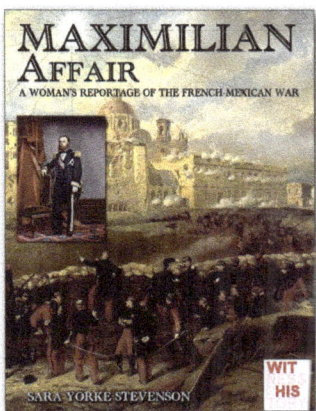

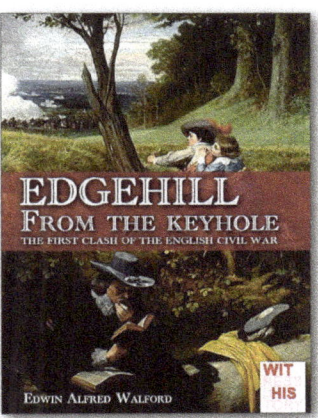

www.ingramcontent.com/pod-product-compliance
Lightning Source LLC
Chambersburg PA
CBHW041145120626
46547CB00020B/3111